R. Dunkerley.

F. II. B.

A SCOTTISH HISTORY
FOR TODAY

Title Page

THE 'RIDING' OF THE SCOTTISH PARLIAMENT

BOOK TWO

A Scottish History for Today

IAN GOULD
D.F.C., M.A.
formerly Principal Teacher of History, Broxburn High School

JOHN THOMPSON
M.A., Ph.D.
Rector of Madras College St. Andrews

Illustrated by John Mackay

John Murray

Reprinted September 1959
Reprinted January 1961

Printed in Great Britain by
Butler & Tanner Ltd., Frome and London
and published by John Murray (Publishers) Ltd.

Foreword

THIS text-book is the second of a series of three written for pupils in the three-year secondary courses in Scottish schools. The authors have endeavoured to write simply and have deliberately cut out a good deal of the tedious political and dynastic information which often discourages pupils from taking an interest in history. In its place they have tried to give some account of the great events outside Scotland which have influenced the growth of the nation, in the hope that pupils will learn how close and long-standing are Scotland's ties with Europe and the New World.

The first volume of the series set out to tell the story of Scotland, against its world background, up to the end of the sixteenth century. This book carries the story up to the present day. This plan is designed to ensure that the many secondary pupils who leave school before they have completed their third year take with them a knowledge of the whole story of the nation. In the third volume the authors supplement and expand some of the work of the second volume, treating things topically rather than chronologically, and include much that is often separately handled as 'Civics' or 'Citizenship'. All three books are divided into sections, each corresponding to a term's work.

Inevitably in many schools some classes are taught history by teachers who are not specialists. To make this series more useful to them the authors are preparing a teachers' handbook containing lists of sources and other helpful material.

Each book is illustrated as lavishly as possible. The captions are brief, deliberately, for the illustrations are closely married to the text and should usually be fully intelligible without further explanation. Some of the drawings contain much detail: from these the fullest value will be derived with the help of notes in the teachers' handbook. The exercises at the end of each chapter have been arranged in order of increasing difficulty.

The illustrator, John Mackay, has worked very closely with the authors and has succeeded in expressing graphically ideas and actions which are difficult to express verbally. The authors again wish to acknowledge their indebtedness to him. They also wish to record the help they have received from the officials of the Royal Scottish Museum, the National Museum of Antiquities, the National Portrait Gallery, the United Services Museum, the Wellcome Historical Medical Library, the Imperial War Museum, and the City Libraries of Edinburgh and Glasgow. Mrs. Joan Stewart read the manuscript, suggested many improvements, and gave valuable advice throughout the preparation of the book. The manuscript was also read from the Catholic standpoint by the Rev. Fr. Gordon, H. Toner, Esq., headmaster of Holy Cross Academy, and others, and from the Presbyterian point of view by the Rev. Campbell Ferenbach and the Rev. Robert Henderson, D.S.O. Their helpful criticism has been greatly appreciated.

Acknowledgements

The authors express their thanks to the following who have kindly permitted the reproduction of copyright photographs. The figures in brackets refer to the plate numbers in this book.

A. G. Ingram Ltd. (*1*); Ministry of Works (*2*); U.S. Information Service (*3*); Aerofilms Ltd. (*4*); John Mackay Esq. (*5 and 6*); the Editor, *Life and Work* (*7*); Paul Popper Ltd. (*8*); Mount Everest Foundation (*9*); Royal Scottish Museum (*10—upper*, *11—upper*, *13*, *14*); North British Locomotive Co. Ltd. (*10—lower*); Jaguar Cars Ltd. (*11—lower*); Director of the Science Museum, London (*12—Wright aeroplane*); The Royal Aeronautical Society (*12—'R34'*); Scottish Aviation Ltd. (*12—'Twin Pioneer'*); De Havilland Aircraft Co. (*12—'Comet'*); Medical Superintendent, Aberdeen Royal Infirmary (*15*); Messrs. T. Hedley & Co. Ltd. (*16*); Associated Press (*17*); U.K. Atomic Energy Authority (*18*); Central Press (*19*); Imperial War Museum (*20*, *22*, *23*, *25*, *26*, *27*); Exclusive News Agency (*21*) Kemsley Picture Service (*24*); James M. Wilson Esq. (*28*).

Contents

Part One

OLD WORLD AND NEW

Part Two

LIFE AND WORK

Part Three

WAR AND PEACE

Illustrations

DRAWINGS IN TEXT

MAPS AND PLANS

PLATES

These are arranged between pages 172 and 173

Part One

OLD WORLD AND NEW

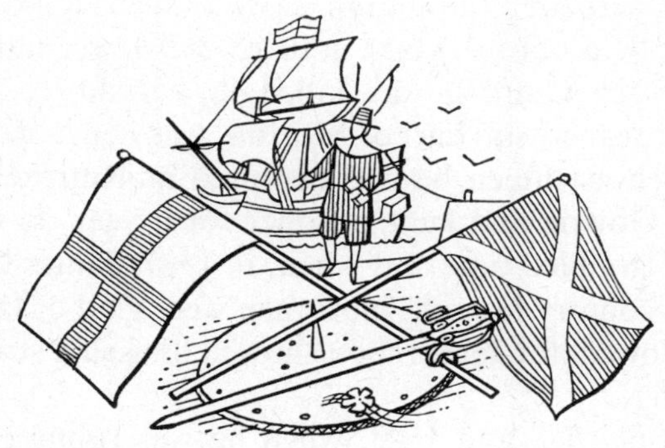

I

James VI and His Troubles

WHEN Mary Queen of Scots was forced to give up her throne and was imprisoned in Loch Leven castle her only son became king. At this time—in 1567—James was still a baby. Obviously he could not rule the country himself, and this hard task had to be done for him by a regent, a noble who ruled in the king's name. The Earl of Moray was the first of these regents, but his regency was short. Many of the nobles still supported Mary, and the ambitious nobles knew that if they controlled the young king they would control Scotland. The Hamiltons struck first: one of their men hid behind some washing in Linlithgow and shot the regent as he was passing through the town. For this crime a great man was to pay with his life. The last Roman Catholic archbishop of St. Andrews was a Hamilton and when Moray's friends caught him they hanged him.

So it went on. Edinburgh castle, under Kirkcaldy of Grange, held out for Mary until 1573. The second regent, the Earl of Lennox, was killed in a fight at Stirling. Another regent, the Earl of Morton, was beheaded. When the king was fifteen he was captured at Ruthven by the Earl of Gowrie and kept prisoner for a year. It was certainly a troubled time and when, in 1587, James began to rule the country himself, most men were glad of the peace that followed, for James soon showed himself a strong and able king.

Between 1587 and 1603, when he was ruling Scotland from Edinburgh, he did his utmost to bring back law and order. For example, he divided Scotland into four districts, and for each district he appointed two royal judges who had to go round their district twice a year and try all the criminals brought before them by the sheriffs. Of course the judges were not very successful in the far-away Highlands or on the Borders where local chiefs were still too strong, but in eastern and western Scotland they did much good. Even the Macgregors, one of the most unruly clans, learned that their plunderings should stop after the clan was outlawed. From his early troubles in Scotland, James learned one lesson: that unless the king was strong, the country suffered.

James had also to try to bring peace to the kirk. You will remember that both in Scotland and in England

Protestant churches were set up at the Reformation; but in both countries many things had still to be decided. How were these new churches to be ruled? What kind of services were to be held? In England at first the answer had been to change as little as possible. The Church of England was still governed by bishops and archbishops, though they were now appointed by the queen: this is why it was called an episcopal church. The service was in English, but most of the English prayer-book was translated from the Latin of the Roman Catholic service. In Scotland, John Knox had tried to set up churches like Calvin's at Geneva, so that Scots churches were later governed by kirk-sessions chosen by the congregation. The service, too, was much simpler, consisting mostly of preaching. This kind of church, where there are elders, was called a Presbyterian church, because *presbyteros* is the Greek word for an elder.

But John Knox knew that in Scotland immediately after the Reformation it would be unwise to do without men to supervise the new churches. These men, who did some of the work once done by bishops, were called superintendents. When Morton was regent he appointed bishops again, and it seemed as if the Scottish and English Churches would both grow up in the same way. But those people who wanted a Presbyterian Church were very strong and soon found a great leader in Andrew Melville. His *Second Book of Discipline* of 1578 urged them to set up Presbyterian churches, without bishops, all over Scotland.

The Presbyterians were so strong that at first the king had to agree, unwillingly. He did not like Melville, and the idea of a church in which ordinary people could choose their ministers and elders was a very strange one at that time. But he waited, and in 1602 he restored the bishops again and allowed them to sit in Parliament. For the rest of his reign James tried slowly and carefully to make the Church of Scotland like the Church of England.

In other ways, too, James worked to unite the two countries. His great chance came in 1603 when Elizabeth, the Queen of England, died leaving no children. James was her nearest heir. Scotland and England were joined under one king and James VI of Scotland became James I of England also. The long wars between the countries were over and the heir of Robert Bruce was crowned King of England.

You must notice carefully what happened: both countries had the same king but they were still separate countries. Scotland still kept her own army, her own navy, her own Parliament. No laws made by the English Parliament applied to Scotland. When James went to London, he ruled Scotland through his Privy Council, a number of nobles and bishops appointed by the king. They could

make rules which had to be obeyed as if they were Acts of Parliament.

He set off on the long journey to London with high hopes both of enjoying the wealth of England and of using his new power to make peace in Europe. He soon found that things were not so easy in England. Under Elizabeth, England had begun a war against the great power of Spain. At first all had gone well: English seamen such as Sir Francis Drake made successful attacks on Spanish colonies in America and on the Spanish treasure ships. The great fleet which the Spaniards sent to carry soldiers into England in 1588, the Great Armada, was smashed by English ships and finally scattered by a great storm which blew them northwards. (One of them, returning to Spain round the north of Scotland, was sunk in Tobermory Bay.) After 1588 English attacks on Spain and Spanish ships were not so successful. To make matters worse, in Ireland there was a rising against the English and Elizabeth had to send troops there. So James found that as King of England he was at war with Spain and had a rebellion in Ireland to put

JAMES VI CROSSING THE BORDER, 1603

down. He at once made peace with Spain and was soon able to crush the Irish rebellion, later sending many Scots to settle in northern Ireland, in Ulster.

The wars and the rebellion had cost a great deal of money. James found that the English Parliament would

COMMUNION TODAY—PRESBYTERIAN

not give him the necessary money very readily. In fact, he found that in England Parliament wanted to have more power. To James, who had learned in Scotland that only a strong king could make a peaceful country, the power of the English Parliament seemed much too great. He was to have many quarrels with his parliaments.

There was trouble about religion. You will remember

how some Roman Catholic plotters employed Guy Fawkes to try to blow up Parliament on November 5th, 1604. Guy Fawkes was caught before he fired his gunpowder, and ever since then the cellars have been searched before Parliament meets. Have you ever wondered what made these

COMMUNION TODAY—EPISCOPALIAN

men try to blow up Parliament? They were trying to protest against the harsh laws against Roman Catholics which had been made when England was at war with Spain.

Much more serious was the trouble with the Puritans. These were men and women who thought that the Church of England was too much like the Roman Catholic Church. They wanted to do away with the white surplices of the clergymen and to make the Church of England more like Calvin's church in its services. Many of them wanted to do away with bishops and with the prayer-book. Some wanted to make the Church of England Presbyterian; others wanted to make each congregation independent. All agreed in being very strict in their behaviour and in studying the Bible very carefully.

Because the Presbyterian party in Scotland was so strong, these English Puritans hoped that James would support them, but they were soon disappointed. James called a meeting of the Puritans and the leaders of the Church of England to his palace at Hampton Court in 1604. There he made it very plain that the Church of England was to keep its bishops and its prayer-book. The Puritans were dissatisfied. A few left England for Holland, and after some years there they then sailed to America where they set up a new colony. But the great majority stayed in England to cause James's son much trouble later on.

From the Hampton Court Conference there was one memorable result: a new translation of the Bible was made, the Authorised Version, which we still use today. When the translators had finished their work, they wrote a letter to James which you will find printed in your own Bible.

We have read about many things in this chapter. Perhaps we should try to say very briefly what James's chief troubles were, because they were to be very important later on:

1. In Scotland a large number of Presbyterians disliked the episcopal church James had set up.

2. In England, Parliament was trying to make itself stronger.
3. In England, too, a large number of people were Puritans and wanted to change the Church of England.

THINGS TO DO

1. Some of the words used in this chapter have very special meanings. Make quite sure before you go on that you understand what 'Presbyterian', 'Episcopal' and 'Puritan' mean.

2. Why do you think James was so much against the Puritans in England?

3. A number of ministers, led by Andrew Melville, went to Falkland Palace to discuss church affairs with James VI. Read carefully what happened there and you will understand why James disliked the Presbyterian Church so much:

> 'The King used his authoritie in maist crabbit and colerik manner, yit Mr Andro bore him down, calling the king bot "God's sillie vassall"; and, taking him by the sleive, sayes this: "Sir, as divers tymes befor, sa now again, I maun tell you, thair is twa Kings and twa Kingdoms in Scotland. Thair is Chryst Jesus the King and his Kingdom the Kirk, whase subject King James the Saxt is, and of whase Kingdom nocht a King, nor a lord, nor a heid, bot a member!'

4. Look at the pictures on pages 6–7. What differences do you notice between the two churches and ministers?

5. Try to find out all you can about England in the reign of Queen Elizabeth. Why was she so popular? Who were some of the great men who lived in her time?

2

Charles I and the Civil War

In 1625 James VI died and his son Charles I became King of Scotland and England. With the kingdoms he also took over all his father's troubles. During his reign he quarrelled with the churches in both countries, with Parliament in England and with the gentry in Scotland. In the end, after a bitter civil war, he was defeated and executed by his English opponents. Let us look first at his troubles in England.

When he became king, England was at war with Spain. Soon Charles was involved in war with France too. With the wars we need not concern ourselves: the English forces were not successful. The important thing to notice is that these wars, like all wars, cost money. Charles could get money, legally, only by asking the English Parliament for it; and Parliament was not very willing to vote extra taxes. Members insisted that the king should agree to certain proposals called the 'Petition of Right'. He was not to impose taxes unless Parliament agreed, nor imprison men illegally. Charles agreed to this in 1628 but still Parliament was not willing to give him enough money. Finally Charles decided to rule without Parliament, raising the money by reviving long-forgotten laws. For example, he began to fine heavily all those who had at any time added parts of the royal forest to their lands. All those who believed that Parliament should have a great part in governing the country turned against him.

With the Puritans Charles made himself even more unpopular than his father had been. His archbishop of Canterbury, Archbishop Laud, felt that there was no reason why churches and church services should be plain or severe. He and Charles began to bring back many of the seemly things which had been lost at the Reformation. Churches were brightened with stained-glass windows and paint, the ministers were made to wear white surplices and organs were used again in the churches. The Puritans suspected—quite wrongly—that Charles and Laud were trying to make the Church Roman Catholic again. Many of them were rich landowners and merchants in close touch with members of Parliament.

All this meant that Charles managed to turn both Puritans and Parliament against him during the first ten years of his reign. The troubles in Scotland were to give them the means of destroying the king, for there he was no more successful.

* * *

Charles had been born in Dunfermline, but had spent so little time in Scotland that he did not really know anything about the people. The tragedy is that he fell out with both the Church and the gentry when he was trying to do his best for the country.

His quarrel with the gentry came over church lands. The Catholic Church had held a great deal of land in Scotland. After the Reformation in 1560 this land did not go to the

Protestant Church, for most of it was taken by the nobles and gentry. This left the Protestant Church very poor, and Charles proposed that this land should be taken from the nobles and gentry and used to help the Church. An Act of Parliament—the Act of Revocation—was drawn up to do this, but there was such an outcry that Charles had to give way and allow the nobles and gentry to keep the land after they had paid a small sum of money. Charles had failed to help the Church and had made enemies of many of the powerful lairds who from now on were ready to do anything to weaken his power.

Trouble in the Church gave them their chance. You will remember that James VI had made the Church episcopalian. In its services, however, the Church was still very much like the Presbyterian Church of today. Charles made up his mind to change this and make the service more like that of the Church of England. Two Scottish bishops drew up a prayer-book for the king to approve. Charles liked it and ordered it to be used in the churches in Scotland, but it was badly received. Men said that it had been written by Laud, the Archbishop of Canterbury, and that it was a Roman Catholic service book. When it was first used in St. Giles' Kirk, Edinburgh, there was a riot and the Dean of Edinburgh was attacked by the congregation. Worse was to follow for Charles. All those who disliked the idea of changes in the service signed a statement saying that they would resist to the end any attempt to make Scotland Roman Catholic again. All over the country and especially south of the Forth, men signed this statement, which we now call the National Covenant, in the year 1638.

In the same year Charles called a General Assembly of

the Church to meet in Glasgow. To it there came not only ministers but elders—many of them powerful lairds. This Assembly deposed the bishops and declared Scotland to be a Presbyterian country. This was open rebellion and Charles gathered an army and marched north to put it down. In Scotland men were not idle and soon a strong army was raised to meet Charles: it was commanded by Alexander Leslie, who had learned his soldiering in the Swedish army. Charles's army was made up of untrained, unwilling soldiers. Sooner than risk a defeat, he made a treaty with the Scots. Next year, 1640, he tried again to crush Scotland—with even less success. This time the Scots defeated his army and occupied Newcastle.

These two short wars of 1639 and 1640, the Bishops' Wars, had cost money. To get more money Charles was forced to recall his English Parliament. That Parliament —the Long Parliament—set to work to gain control of the country. Charles's advisers, Laud, the Archbishop of Canterbury, and Wentworth, Earl of Strafford, were arrested and executed; the special courts by which Charles had governed were abolished; Charles's power was limited in every way. By 1642 it was plain to both sides that either king or Parliament must rule. Only war would decide, and king and Parliament began to raise armies.

In English history this war is called the 'Civil War'. Here we need not worry about details of the battles. It will be enough if we remember the nicknames of the two sides —Cavaliers or king's men and Roundheads or Parliament's men; and the name of the great leader on Parliament's side—Oliver Cromwell, who commanded a splendid force of soldiers called Ironsides.

The Scots came into the war on both sides. In 1643 a treaty was made with the English Parliament, which was then desperate for help, a treaty called the Solemn League and Covenant. In this the Scots promised to send soldiers to help Parliament on condition that England was made Presbyterian after the king was defeated. As a result of

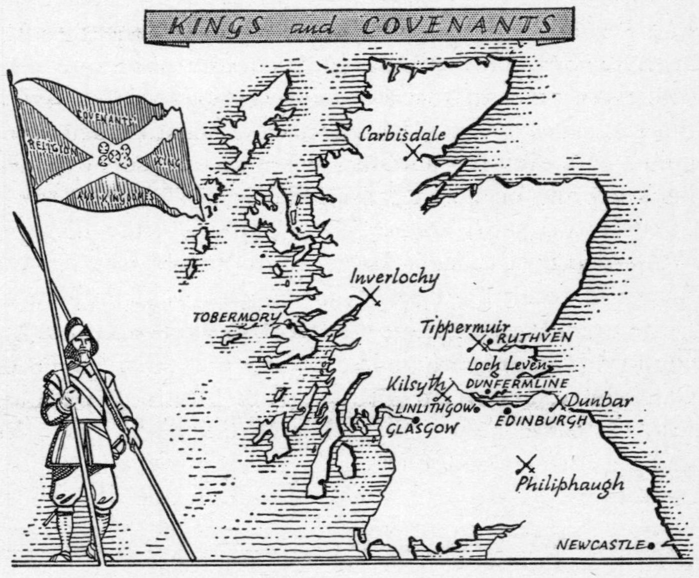

this treaty some Scots soldiers fought against the king in England, while in Scotland others fought on his side. The Marquis of Montrose raised an army of Highland and Irish soldiers in 1644 to help the king, and at first he was very successful. At Tippermuir, near Perth, at Inverlochy, in the west and at Kilsyth he defeated the king's enemies. All Scotland was his and the way seemed open for him to come to the help of the king in England, but it was too late. Already a Scots army under Sir David Leslie had left England and was marching to meet Montrose. Near Selkirk, at Philiphaugh, in 1645 the two armies met. Montrose's army was defeated and scattered, and the king had

MONTROSE PASSING MORAY HOUSE IN THE CANONGATE

no hope now from Scotland. In 1646 he was forced to surrender to the Scots army in England.

When the king surrendered, the war for England was over. Parliament appeared to have won. In fact the army under Oliver Cromwell had won and the army insisted that Charles should die. In January 1649 the headsman killed him outside his banqueting hall in Whitehall.

The Scots had no say in his death. Indeed Scotland was horrified at the news and at once invited Charles's son, Charles II, to come over to Scotland. Charles sent Montrose over first. His army was defeated at Carbisdale in Ross-shire and Montrose was captured and executed in Edinburgh. Later the boy king came over to be crowned, but before the ceremony could be performed, Cromwell came north with an army. He knew that in England many people supported the king and would fight again for him. If Charles ruled in Scotland all these English supporters would be encouraged. Cromwell, therefore, hurried—trying first to take Edinburgh. He failed and was forced back on his base at Dunbar, followed by the Scots army which kept to the high ground along the Lammermuirs. At Dunbar Cromwell appeared to be trapped. The Scots army on the hills prevented him from marching south, and he could not hope to get all his men out by sea. But the Scots blundered and came down to attack him too soon. Cromwell's battle-trained Ironsides were too good and drove the Scots from the field.

Next year, 1651, Charles II made his last attempt. The way south from Stirling was still open, and Charles led his remaining Scots army southwards into England, with Cromwell coming swiftly behind. At Worcester Cromwell won his final victory and Charles had to flee to France. Cromwell and his army were masters of Britain.

The next nine years were prosperous and peaceful ones. Scotland and England were joined into one country, one Commonwealth, under Cromwell as Protector. Scottish merchants could now trade freely with England and the English lands overseas. An English army maintained law and order in Scotland. Even religious quarrels were ended.

But this union was not to last. When Cromwell died in 1658 his son succeeded him for a short time. Finally in 1660 Charles II was called back to be king of both Scotland and England.

THINGS TO DO

1. Make quite sure that you understand what these words mean: gentry, laird, tax, surplice, dean.

2. Draw two columns in your notebook, one for Scotland and one for England. Write down very shortly how Charles made himself unpopular in each country.

3. Try to find out more about the Marquis of Montrose and Oliver Cromwell.

4. Why is the struggle between king and Parliament so important? What had it to do with the kind of government we have today?

5. Think of as many reasons as you can why Scotland would benefit from being joined with England under Cromwell. Write them down one by one.

6. Write down in a few sentences why these were important: Petition of Right; Act of Revocation; Solemn League and Covenant; Battle of Worcester.

7. Here is part of the National Covenant signed by Scots in most parts of the country. Notice how they swore to protect their protestant religion and be loyal to their king:

> 'We promise, and sweare by the Great Name of the Lord our God, to continue in the Profession and Obedience of the Foresaid Religion: That we shall defend the same, and resist all these contrary errours according to the uttermost of that

> power that God hath put in our hands, all the dayes of our life: and in like manner with the same heart, we declare before God and Men, that we have no intention nor desire to attempt any thing that may turne to the dishonour of God, or to the diminution of the king's greatnesse and authority: But on the contrary, we promise and sweare, that we shall, to the uttermost of our power, with our meanes and lives, stand to the defence of our dread Soveraigne, the Kings Majesty.'

The Covenanters soon found, however, that they had to choose between their king and their Presbyterian religion. As you have read, they chose their religion, and fought against their king to defend it.

3
The Covenanters

In 1660 Charles II came back to London from France. Everywhere people rejoiced, for Cromwell's rule had been

A CONVENTICLE

strict and men looked forward to a little more freedom. In Edinburgh the fountains ran with wine and there were celebrations everywhere. Scotland was independent again.

This rejoicing did not last long, however. The first parliament Charles summoned—the Drunken Parliament men called it—passed an Act called the Rescissory Act which repealed all laws made since 1633. In other words, all the laws abolishing episcopacy were cancelled and the Church of Scotland became again a Church governed by bishops. Charles was too wise to go further: he made no attempt to change the form of service. But the bishops were unpopular in many parts of the country, especially in the south-west. Indeed, almost a third of the ministers left their churches rather than work under the bishops, and began to hold open-air services, conventicles, in the hills. These men were called Covenanters. Then in 1666 a rebellion against the government began in Dumfries among these Covenanters. They marched on Edinburgh but were caught and defeated at Rullion Green in the Pentlands by Tam Dalziel, a Scots soldier who had served in the Russian army. Many prisoners were taken, and a few were hanged, some being tortured first with the 'boot' or the 'thumb-screws'. (Torturing was still legal in Scotland, as in most

European countries, but it had rather gone out of fashion.)

For the next thirteen years there was an uneasy quiet. The conventicles still went on and the government tried hard to stop them, fining lairds who allowed conventicles to take place on their lands, and billeting Highland soldiers (who were not too careful to keep the eighth commandment) in the villages of the south-west.

In 1679 there was more violence. The Archbishop of St. Andrews, James Sharp, had made himself unpopular both by becoming a bishop and by the energy with which he tried to enforce the laws against conventicles. He was dragged from his coach on Magus Muir outside St. Andrews and there foully murdered by a party of twelve men. A month later the members of a conventicle on Loudoun Hill in Ayrshire were caught by government troops. They turned to fight and defeated the troops at Drumclog, but their victory was short-lived. Before the month was over the Covenanters had been defeated and scattered at Bothwell Brig.

Yet Bothwell Brig was not the end. The Covenanters, though few in numbers now, found new leaders, especially

THE MURDER OF ARCHBISHOP SHARP

Richard Cameron. In 1684 they published a declaration of open war against the government, the 'Apologetical Declaration', threatening death to all enemies of the Covenant. This made things much easier for the government troops. In future, any prisoners were asked whether they would take an oath against the 'Apologetical Declaration'. If they refused to take the oath they could be shot out of hand as traitors. The years after the Declaration appeared are called the 'Killing Time'.

* * *

In England Charles was equally welcome in 1660 and there men were slower to turn against him. The Church of England was restored as the church of the country and the Puritans driven from power; Parliament was restored; and all the Puritan laws against merry-making were repealed. The first few years were very happy ones, but even then there were many discontented men. The Puritans were harshly treated in many ways and were waiting their chance to oppose the king. Many country gentlemen who had supported Charles I faithfully found that Charles II would not or could not help them. Besides, the great and growing strength of Catholic France, which was soon to be the greatest Power in the world, frightened those who saw how friendly Charles was with France. In fact, Charles had become a secret Roman Catholic while he was in exile and was to do all he could to help both his fellow-Catholics and France.

In 1670 a secret treaty was signed with France by which Charles undertook to make England Roman Catholic if

Louis XIV, the King of France, would help him with men and money. The treaty was secret but Parliament heard a rumour of it and passed a Test Act forbidding anyone except members of the Church of England to hold any government post. For example, they could not be officers in the army or the navy. All those who opposed Charles in Parliament came together to form a political party called the Whig party. Those who supported the king formed the Tory party. When the king died in 1685 the Whig party was strong. His brother, who succeeded him as James VII and II, was to fall foul of the party and lose his throne.

James started off with a serious disadvantage: he was an open Roman Catholic. He soon made it plain that he would not be content until England was Roman Catholic. (Even in Scotland the church at Holyrood was restored and used for Roman Catholic services.) In spite of the Test Act, Roman Catholics were given commissions in the army. You see why this is so important? If the king can ignore the laws of Parliament it means that he is all-powerful. James also tried to give Roman Catholics the right to worship freely by drawing up a Declaration of Indulgence permitting all men to worship as they pleased. He ordered the clergy to read this from their pulpits, and when many refused to do so, he imprisoned seven of the bishops, though the courts later set them free. When a son was born to James and his Catholic wife men feared that there would be a long line of Catholic kings. Some of the leading men invited William of Orange, the protestant prince of the Netherlands who had married James's daughter Mary, to come over and rule.

In 1688 William landed in Devonshire and was greeted

with enthusiasm all the way to London. James fled to France. William and Mary were crowned King and Queen of England.

Parliament decided that there should never again be kings who were too strong and could override the law. A number of laws were passed to make sure that the king's power was cut down. The most important of these is still called the Bill of Rights, though it became a law. (Notice that in the language of Parliament a law or act is called a 'bill' before it has been passed.) By this Bill of Rights the king was forbidden to alter laws without the permission of Parliament, to keep an army without permission of Parliament, or to raise money without permission of Parliament. It was also laid down that no one who was a Roman Catholic, or was married to a Roman Catholic, could become king or queen. This was in 1689. Later, in 1701, Parliament went further and laid down who should succeed William. From now on the rulers of England had to call Parliament often and rule by its advice.

In 1689, too, the Puritans were at last set free by the Toleration Act, to worship as they pleased.

In England the coming of William and Mary and the driving out of James II is called the 'Glorious Revolution'.

* * *

In Scotland William and Mary did not find things quite so easy. The news that they had landed was welcome to all who did not like the Episcopal Church, for William was a Calvinist. But many people in Scotland, especially in the north, were still faithful to King James and the Episcopal

Church. They found a leader in Graham of Claverhouse, the 'Bonny Dundee' of the song, who had been one of the commanders in the wars against the Covenanters. He soon raised a Highland army and in his first battle defeated the troops of the Scottish government. This was at Killiecrankie, where the Highlanders made a wild charge down the steep hillside above the River Garry. In the battle Dundee himself was killed, and when his men were held up at Dunkeld on their march south, they lost heart without his leadership and slipped off home. From now on, for nearly a hundred years, Scotland was to be divided into two groups, those who wanted the Stuart kings back again—the Jacobites—and those who did not.

While Dundee was raising his army in the north, Parliament in Edinburgh prepared a 'Claim of Right', a long document listing all King James's misdeeds and declaring that William and Mary were to be the rulers of Scotland. The following year the Church of Scotland was made Presbyterian again, and it has remained so ever since.

* * *

By 1690, then, William and Mary were firmly in control of both countries, but their power was limited in England by the Bill of Rights and in Scotland by a more active Parliament than ever before. In England there was religious peace. In Scotland the Presbyterian Church was restored, but many people still remained Roman Catholic or Episcopalian.

THINGS TO DO

1. Make sure you know the meanings of these words: legal, billet, oath, repeal, treaty, bill (of Parliament).

2. See if you can learn the song *Bonny Dundee.*

3. Divide a page of your notebook in two. Head one side 'Scotland' and the other 'England'. Write down briefly how Charles II made himself unpopular in each country.

4. In the past three chapters you have read a good deal about Parliament. Begin now to collect examples from your newspaper of the work Parliament does today.

5. Write short paragraphs to explain the importance of: Rescissory Act; Apologetical Declaration; Test Act; Bill of Rights.

6. Here is part of the Claim of Right. Read it carefully, and you will see how James had been using his power. Parliament was determined that the king would not do these things again.

The Estates of the Kingdom of Scotland declare:

> That by the law of the Kingdom no Papist can be King or Queen of this Realm.
>
> That the giving gifts or grants for raising of money without the consent of Parliament is contrary to law.
>
> That imprisoning persons without expressing the reasons thereof, and delaying putting them to trial, is contrary to law.
>
> That using torture without evidence, or in ordinary crimes, is contrary to law.
>
> That prelacy [that is, government with bishops] hath been a great trouble to this nation and ought to be abolished.
>
> That for the redress of all grievances and for the amending, strengthening and preserving of the laws, Parliaments ought to be frequently called, and allowed to sit, and the freedom of speech and debate secured to the members.

4

The Union of Scotland and England

AFTER James VI became King of England in 1603, Scotland and England had the same king but were quite separate in other ways, except during the time of Cromwell. The kings remained in England and governed Scotland by a Privy Council in Edinburgh. It was a clumsy way of governing but it worked fairly well until William and Mary came to the throne. The difficulties which followed made many of the ablest men in both countries think that a closer union was needed. Finally in 1707 the two countries were joined to form Great Britain.

What were these difficulties? You remember Bonny Dundee? He was defeated and killed and his army was stopped at Dunkeld, but that did not make the Highlanders any more friendly to the government of William and Mary. To make sure that they did not rise again for James two things were done: a strong fort was built on the west, Fort William; and the chiefs were made to take an oath to be loyal to the new government—before January 1st, 1692. Most of them did so, though some left it very late. One of these was MacIan, the chief of the Macdonalds of Glencoe. He came to Fort William to take the oath, but found that he had to go to Inverary. The journey in a snowy winter was a long one and he came too late. At once the government in Edinburgh saw its chance to make an example which would terrify others. The Secretary of State, the Master of Stair, gave orders to Campbell of Glenlyon to wipe out the Macdonalds of Glencoe. For twelve days the Campbell soldiers stayed with the Macdonalds, then on February 13th they rose and killed the

chief and about thirty others. It was a treacherous murder, and men knew that although Campbell soldiers had done the killing they were acting on the orders of William's government in Edinburgh.

Worse was to follow. The years 1696 to 1700 were years of famine in many parts of Scotland. Wet summers made it impossible to save much of the harvest. People were so hungry that we hear of parents selling some of their children as bond servants (more or less slaves) to America in order to buy bread for the rest of the family: for as corn became scarce the price rose and poor people could not buy it.

In the middle of these hungry years William Paterson, a Scot who had made his fortune in the West Indies and had founded the Bank of England, was busy with what seemed a brilliant idea to increase the wealth of Scotland and provide new land for Scots to settle in. The English East India Company had the sole right to trade with India, and shareholders of this company were becoming very rich. England, too, had many colonies in America and the West Indies, while Scotland had nothing to show except an unsuccessful attempt to colonise Nova Scotia. Paterson's idea, then, was to found a Scottish company which would carry on trade with Africa and India and would set up a Scottish colony at Darien, near the present Panama Canal. The idea was good, but Paterson did not take sufficient account of the difficulties—disease, the Spaniards who owned Darien, and King William.

THE ARMS OF THE DARIEN COMPANY

Originally the plan had been to set up a company half English and half Scots, but the English East India Company was so jealous that the English Parliament stopped English merchants from taking part. In 1696 the company was made purely a Scottish one with its head office in Edinburgh. For the next two years there was a great bustle: ships were bought, colonists chosen, and goods to trade with got ready. (Some of the goods for trade with the natives were rather odd—wigs, for example.) In 1698 the first fleet set sail from Leith to found New Caledonia in Darien. The ships were *St. Andrew*, *Caledonia*, *Unicorn*, *Dolphin*, and *Endeavour*. A good deal of the wealth of Scotland was invested in the fleet and there were high hopes of success.

In Darien at first all went well. A fort was built, the Spaniards were driven off, and the Indians were friendly. There was fever, of course, and some colonists died, but that was to be expected. Disaster began when the colonists sent a ship to the English colony of Jamaica for extra food. There the Governor told them that King William had ordered him not to help the colonists. It seemed difficult to believe that their own king had ordered this. We know now that William wanted to stay friendly with Spain at all costs and he was afraid that Spain would blame him for the settlement at Darien. But the colonists could not understand, and it seemed useless to carry on. They re-embarked and set sail for home, but only one ship, the *Caledonia*, reached Scotland.

Another expedition was sent out in 1699. This one, after beating a small force of Spaniards, was forced to surrender by a larger Spanish army. It was the end of this

Scots colony and all the money spent on it had been lost. King William was blamed.

There was one bright event. A Scottish ship of the company's was sent to trade with Africa and came back with a cargo of ivory, rice and gold. From this gold the last Scots gold coins were minted: pistoles worth £12 and half-pistoles worth £6. (Each Scots pound was worth 1*s*. 8*d*. in English money.) Another ship, the *Speedy Return*, was sent to India. It did not return, and we can see from what followed how bitter the Scots were feeling towards the English. Shortly afterwards the English ship, the *Worcester*, came into Leith and the story went round that this ship had captured the *Speedy Return*. There was no truth in the story but feeling was so strong that the captain of the *Worcester* and two of his officers were hanged on Leith Links as pirates.

Soon Scotland and England were to be even more bitter against each other. In 1701 the English Parliament passed the Act of Settlement which said that when William died the throne should go to Mary's sister Anne. After her the queen was to be a German princess, the Electress Sophia of Hanover, who was descended from James VI. Anne became Queen of England in 1702 and was also recognised as Queen of Scotland. But many Scots thought that they should not be bound by the English Act: for, they asked, why should the English Parliament choose the ruler of Scotland? So the Scots Parliament passed an Act of Security which said that when Anne died Scotland would choose a different ruler from the ruler of England unless Scots merchants received the same trading rights as English ones. To make it plain that the Scots meant business, the Act also permitted the government of Scotland to call men up for training and to put the border in a state of defence.

England was in a dangerous position. She was in the middle of a bitter war with France—the War of the Spanish Succession. There was a serious risk that if the French sent an army to Scotland the Scottish Jacobites would rise

THE SCOTS PARLIAMENT AT WORK

against Queen Anne. The only way to end the danger was to bring the two countries closer together by uniting the parliaments. A number of men, 31 from Scotland and the same number from England, were appointed to make a treaty to unite the two countries. In 1707 the union was complete and the Scots Parliament met for the last time.

It is worth while looking rather closely at this treaty

which ended our existence as a separate nation. In the new parliament of Great Britain Scotland was to have 45 members in the House of Commons and England was to have 512. The Scots lords were to be represented in the House of Lords by 16 lords, chosen by the others at the time of each General Election. The new Parliament was to make laws for all Great Britain, but Scotland was to keep her own laws and her own law courts, as she still does. The great benefit to Scotland was that from now on her merchants could trade freely with England and all the English colonies overseas. English weights and measures were to be used everywhere—a great help to trade—and English money was to be the currency of Great Britain. There was to be a common flag, a Union flag or jack, made by placing the cross of St. George on the saltire of St. Andrew. (It was not quite the same as the present Union Jack. The parts representing the cross of St. Patrick were not included till later.) The Scots army and navy were united with the English to form the Royal Navy and the British Army. Scotland, too, had to take her share of the English National Debt and English taxes. In return she received a sum of £400,000 with which to make up the losses suffered in the Darien scheme. Of course many of these changes took time. Men still talk of bawbees instead of halfpennies; for a long time farmers measured their grain in bolls and chalders, not in bushels and quarters; and the union of the parliaments did not destroy Scotland as a nation. We still think of ourselves as Scots first and Britons second. We know that we are in some mysterious way different from the English. We are still a nation.

Today many people are saying that the Union of 1707

was a mixed blessing and are asking whether it is not possible for Scotland to stay within the British Commonwealth but to have a government of her own again. What do you think?

THINGS TO DO

1. Imagine that you are one of the colonists who came back on the *Caledonia* from Darien. Write a letter to a friend explaining why you decided to come home.

2. If you live near Edinburgh or visit the town make sure you go to see the Parliament Hall (shown in Plate 1) where the Scots Parliament used to meet.

3. Make a note of the reasons why Scotland and England were on such bad terms just before the Union.

4. Write short paragraphs about the Act of Settlement and the Act of Security.

5. Make a list of the main terms of the Act of Union.

6. Why do some people today dislike the Act of Union? Try to make two lists, one showing what Scotland gains from being joined to England, the other showing what she loses.

5

The Highlands and the Jacobite Risings

SO FAR we have treated Scotland as if it were one country in every way. Yet there had always been a division within Scotland, a division between highland and lowland, between Saxon and Celt. North and west of the highland line most people spoke Gaelic and lived as clansmen ruled over by their chiefs. Today the highlands are an empty land, a land of few people and many sheep, except where the Forestry Commission and hydro-electric schemes are creating work. But in 1707 there were many more people living in the highlands.

Their life was a hard one. The soil is usually poor, crops do not grow well, and the rainfall in the west is so heavy that it is difficult to harvest the corn. They lived by growing a little corn, fishing, and rearing cattle on the hills, cattle which were afterwards driven south in enormous numbers to be sold at the annual markets, or trysts, at Crieff, or Falkirk or Carlisle. A bad season's fishing or a wet summer could mean starvation. Because they were so poor many who lived near the lowlands turned to reiving, raiding the lowland farms and driving off cattle. In one of his novels Sir Walter Scott describes this, putting the words into the mouth of a Glasgow merchant, Bailie Nicol Jarvie. 'And mair especially, mony hundreds o' them come down to the borders of the low country, where there's gear to grip, and live by stealing, reiving, lifting cows and the like depredations—a thing deplorable in any Christian country!'

The highlanders were grouped into clans under their chiefs. In theory all members of the clan were of the same name and claimed to be descended from one man. In fact, their names often differed. The tartan cloth which they wore wrapped round themselves like a combined kilt and jacket was not always the same pattern even within the one clan. But, generally, the members of one clan could be distinguished from those of another by their tartan and by the badge they wore in their bonnets. Their weapons of war were old-fashioned but very effective in the hands of brave, fierce men: they did not have a bayonet but carried both musket and broadsword with a round targe to stop the enemies' blows. The chiefs were very powerful. Their word was, in fact, law, for many of them—or rather their stewards—acted as judges and could punish with death.

In this wild land the Presbyterian Church had made little progress. Many of the clans in the Hebrides and the western mainland still kept the Roman Catholic faith, as they still do; many in the north east were strong episcopalians. Few of them liked the Union of 1707 and the idea of being ruled by a London king who supported the Presbyterian Church was hated. They looked to the son of James VII to come over and make himself king again. The highlanders called him James VIII; his enemies called him the 'Old Pretender'.

In 1715 the first chance came to make James king. Queen Anne died in 1714. In her place George, the Elector of Hanover, became king under the terms of the Act of

Settlement. He spoke little English and preferred to live in Hanover. Many who had accepted Queen Anne because she was James VII's daughter did not want this foreigner as king. One of their leaders was the Earl of Mar. He invited the highland chiefs to a hunting party on the Braes of Mar and when they were all gathered together he hoisted the standard of King James and urged the clansmen to follow him and restore their king. Marching south they took Perth easily. Part of the army under Mackintosh of Borlum moved into Fife, crossed the Forth in fishing-boats, and almost seized Edinburgh. At the last moment Mackintosh's men were driven off, and they then marched on to Kelso where they joined the men of the south who had risen for King James. From Kelso the little army went on to invade England, marching south to Preston in Lancashire where it was finally surrounded and forced to surrender.

Meanwhile the Earl of Mar marched slowly on Stirling, the 'gate' which separated highlands and lowlands. His way was barred by the Duke of Argyll, 'Red Colin of the Battles', who commanded the government forces. At Sheriffmuir on the Ochils the two armies met. The right wing of each army broke the left wing of the other. It seemed to be a drawn battle, but Mar had lost, for Argyll held his ground and Mar fell back slowly on Perth, burning the corn and driving off the cattle as he went to stop Argyll's men having them. The king himself came over from France but he was a wet blanket, a cold, distant man who obviously did not expect to win. From Perth the army retreated to Aberdeen. King James took ship again for France; the highlanders were told to scatter; the rising was over.

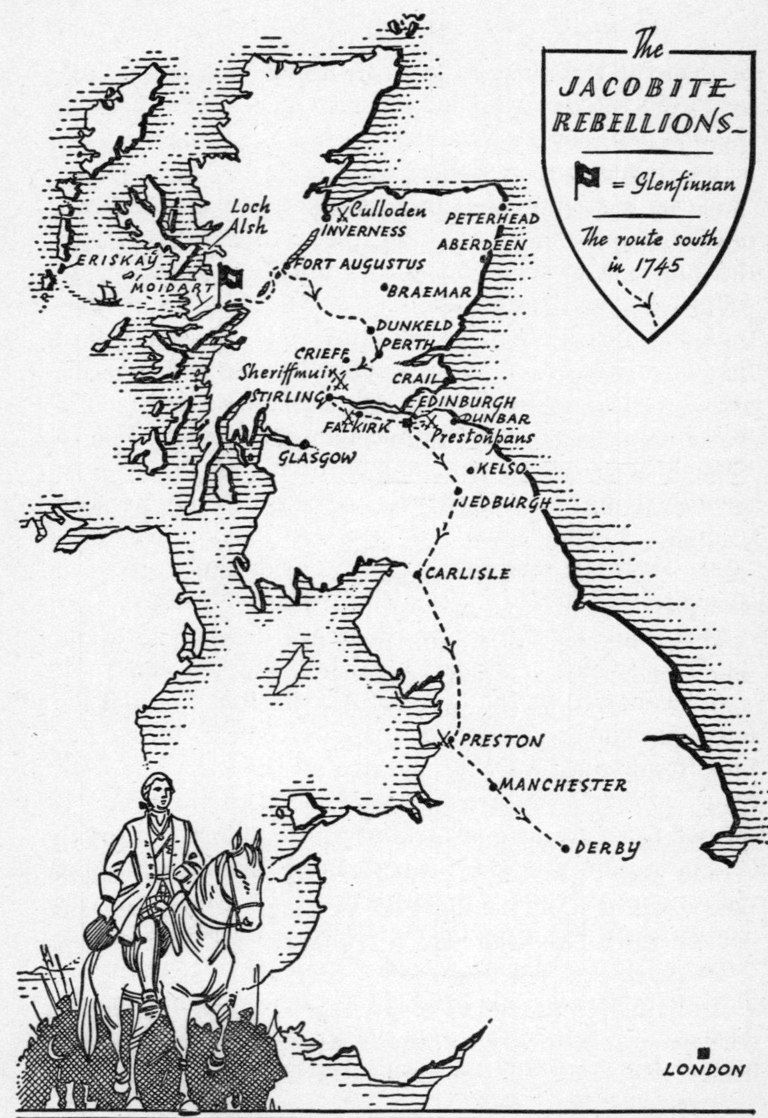
The
JACOBITE
REBELLIONS
= Glenfinnan
The route south
in 1745
Loch
Alsh
Culloden
INVERNESS
PETERHEAD
ABERDEEN
ERISKAY
FORT AUGUSTUS
MOIDART
BRAEMAR
DUNKELD
PERTH
CRIEFF
Sheriffmuir
CRAIL
STIRLING
EDINBURGH
DUNBAR
FALKIRK
Prestonpans
GLASGOW
KELSO
JEDBURGH
CARLISLE
PRESTON
MANCHESTER
DERBY
LONDON

There was another small rising in the highlands in 1719 when the Earl Marischal landed by Loch Alsh with three hundred Spanish troops. This was very soon put down.

The two risings made the government see that something must be done to keep the highlands quiet. In 1725 a Disarming Act was passed to make the clansmen hand in their weapons of war. They handed in useless muskets and rusty swords; the good ones were hidden in the thatch to wait for another day. Companies of soldiers dressed in dark tartan had for some time been raised from the highlands to act as a Watch or armed police force. Later these soldiers were to form one regiment, the Black Watch. Above all the government tried to keep the highlands quiet by building forts and roads along which artillery and supply wagons could move. The chief forts were Fort George and Fort Augustus. These, with Fort William, were meant to guard the Great Glen which divides the highlands. General Wade was the principal road builder, constructing nearly 260 miles of road joining Fort William to Inverness and Inverness to Dunkeld, with a branch from Dalwhinnie to Fort Augustus. The roads were soon to be needed.

A BLACK WATCH SOLDIER IN 1760

In 1745 the highlanders rose for the last time. Britain was then at war with France and a large part of the regular army was serving in Belgium. The French government saw that a Jacobite rising in Scotland would cause great disturbance and perhaps make the British troops withdraw from Belgium. No objection was made in France when Prince Charles Edward, the elder son of James, the Old Pretender, bought two French warships and a stock of weapons to take to Scotland. The young prince, Bonnie Prince Charlie, was very different from his father. He was dashing and brave, and was popular everywhere he went.

One of his ships was forced to turn back. With the other he sailed on to Eriskay in the Hebrides, then crossed to Moidart on the mainland. At first the highland chiefs were slow to join him. Not till Cameron of Lochiel brought in 700 of his Camerons did the others come in any number. Soon his army numbered 2,500 and he felt confident that he could take Scotland, where there were few troops left. On his way south the prince used General Wade's road to take his army towards Stirling. There was no opposition till he came near Edinburgh, and even there he was met merely by two regiments of dragoons who fled at the first shots.

Edinburgh was seized without fighting. Lochiel's men slipped through the Netherbow Port as the gate opened to let a coach through. The prince held court in Holyrood.

Outside Edinburgh the prince had his first battle with government troops. General Cope advanced on Edinburgh through East Lothian and halted at Prestonpans in a strong position, with his flank protected by a marsh. A local guide led the highlanders through the marsh during the night and when the morning mists cleared the highlanders were on firm ground. In one fierce charge Cope's army was scattered and the prince was master of Scotland. The song,

'Hey, Johnnie Cope', which is the reveille of the highland regiments today, reminds us of the victory.

After Prestonpans the prince waited in Edinburgh for six weeks, gathering supplies and recruits for the march on London. During that time the government was hurriedly calling back the army from Belgium and General Wade was sent to hold Newcastle with a large army. The prince decided to follow the western road through Carlisle. Carlisle was captured and the highlanders pressed steadily southwards, through Preston and Manchester to Derby. There the news was bad. The Duke of Cumberland with a large army of regulars lay between Derby and London. The wisest course was to retreat quickly, hold the north of Scotland during the winter, raise more soldiers, and wait for help from France. The prince, reluctantly, decided to do so. On the way north to Inverness a government army was scattered at Falkirk.

So far the highlanders had been successful in every battle or skirmish, but they had not met well-trained regular troops. They soon were to meet them. The Duke of Cumberland's army made its slow way north and came along the coast of the Moray Firth towards Inverness. The highland army tried again a night attack but failed to reach Cumberland's men before daylight and fell back on Culloden Moor. There the last battle of the war was fought. The weary, hungry highlanders charged in vain against Cumberland's steady red-coats: the Royal Artillery broke up their attacks and hastened their retreat; the cavalry turned the retreat into a rout, and the prince was led off the field into hiding. The rising was over.

We must be careful to notice that the victory was won

by a British, not an English, army. Many of the regiments which made up Cumberland's army were Scottish regiments, either regular or, like the Argyll Highlanders, territorial. It had not been a battle of English against highlanders, but of British troops against rebels. That accounts for much of the cruelty which followed when

CULLODEN

wounded men were killed and prisoners were shot. Cumberland earned the name of 'Butcher'.

Culloden was fought in April 1746. Prince Charles was a fugitive until September, when a French ship took him back to France. There was a price of £30,000 on his head, but no one was so mean as to betray him. You remember that for part of this time he was disguised as Betty Burke, the servant of Flora MacDonald?

There was no doubt that the '45 had been a shock to the government, such a shock that after Culloden everything possible was done to keep the highlands quiet in future. For example, the clans were broken up. It was made a serious crime to wear the kilt, or own weapons, or even to play the bagpipe. The chiefs' power was taken away: they could no longer act as judges and try cases in their own courts. The chiefs became simply landowners, lairds as we say, and soon realised that it was more profitable to turn their lands into sheep-farms worked by a few shepherds than to let them out to their clansmen. Many thousands of highlanders had to leave the glens, some to seek work in the lowland towns, others to settle in North America, especially in Canada, so that today Gaelic is spoken by many people in Nova Scotia, and all over Canada are millions of people whose ancestors came from Scotland. In the New World they found richer lands than Scotland, and lived better than if they had remained at home, but nothing can excuse the callousness of some of the highland landowners, especially such men as the Duke of Sutherland, who drove his tenants from his lands and turned vast stretches of the highlands into lands cleared of all except of sheep and deer.

THINGS TO DO

1. There are a great many novels about the Jacobite risings. Here are the titles of three which you should read:

   Kidnapped by R. L. Stevenson
   The New Road by Neil Munro
   Midwinter by John Buchan

2. When you next go to music sing some of the Jacobite

songs—*The Skye Boat Song*; *Wae's me for Prince Charlie*; *Come owre the stream, Charlie*. There are plenty of others in Scots and in Gaelic.

3. Try to find out where the main clans lived. Make a sketch map and mark on it the territories of each.

4. Tell the story of the '45 campaign as if you were a Cameron who had been in it from the beginning.

5. Write down as many reasons as you can why the Jacobite army was so successful at first in the '45.

6

Re-shaping Europe

IT IS very easy for us in Britain to forget that we are part of Europe. The North Sea and the English Channel seem to cut us off completely, but in every way we are really part of Europe and everything that happens there, on the mainland, affects us. This was particularly true in the seventeenth century. Many Scotsmen served in other countries as soldiers of fortune—in the Swedish, Dutch, French, and even Russian, armies. Scots merchants were busy trading with Holland, Poland and north Germany. Moreover, after the Civil War a great many Scots fled to Holland to live there.

Obviously we cannot follow the story of each of the countries of Europe at this time. The most we can do is to look at some of the important happenings, especially at those which are important for the future.

Towards the end of the reign of James VI a great war broke out in Europe, a war which lasted all through the reign of Charles I. This war is usually called the Thirty Years War and it lasted from 1618 to 1648. The lands we call Germany, Sweden, Denmark, Austria, Holland, France and Spain were all drawn into it; there was very great destruction and death from hunger and disease; and when the war ended Europe was exhausted. The fighting began

in what we now call Germany and was then called the Holy Roman Empire. The head of this 'Empire' was the Catholic ruler of Austria. The Empire was broken up into many states such as Prussia, Saxony and the Palatinate, ruled by princes. It also contained states ruled by arch-

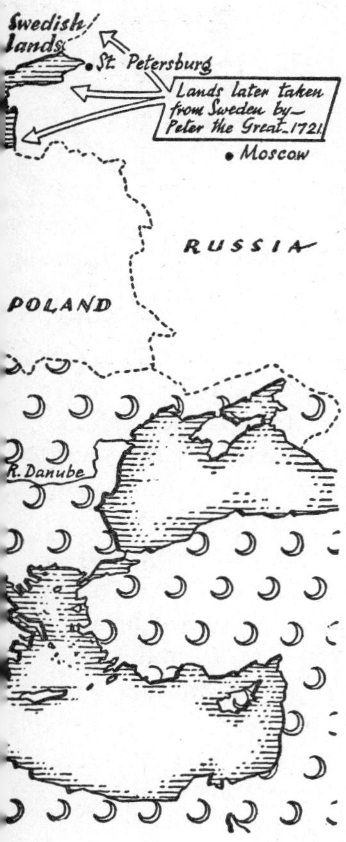

bishops and free towns which governed themselves. Some of these states and towns were Protestant, others were Catholic. All were anxious to keep their own freedom and many disliked the power of the Emperor. So the war was fought partly as a war between Protestants and Catholics, partly as a war of the states against the Emperor.

In Czechoslovakia the people drove out the Emperor's officials and invited the Protestant Elector Palatine to become their king. The Emperor's Catholic armies soon drove the Elector Palatine out of Czechoslovakia and reconquered the country. When the King of Denmark came into the war on the Protestant side he, too, was soon beaten. It seemed as if the power of the Emperor was going to become very great, and as if Germany was going to become Catholic.

The Protestant princes were saved by Sweden. Under their great soldier-king Gustavus Adolphus the Swedish armies, which included many Scottish soldiers of fortune, entered Germany and defeated the Emperor's armies. When Gustavus was killed at Lützen in 1632 the Swedish armies stayed in Germany, helped by money from France. The fact that France came into the war on the Swedish side shows that it was not just a war between Catholics and Protestants. The chief minister in Catholic France was Cardinal Richelieu, who helped the Swedes with money because he hoped that France would become greater if the Emperor was defeated.

The people of Germany suffered very much during the war, because the armies lived off the country. Parties of foragers would scour the countryside taking corn, hay, wheat and animals from the farmers to feed the soldiers and their horses. The farmers were often left to starve; and hungry people catch diseases easily. Hundreds of thousands of civilians died.

When peace came in 1648, the Peace of Westphalia, every one was delighted. For the next hundred years men looked back to this peace as a turning-point in the history of Europe. France and Sweden gained lands from the Empire, and Holland was recognised as an independent country. Within the Empire the states were left more powerful and the Emperor weaker. The wars between Catholic and Protestant were ended. What was not so plain then was that the Empire was left so weak that France became too strong.

During the next sixty years which followed the Peace of Westphalia, France, under her great king Louis XIV, became the greatest power in western Europe. Louis' ambition was to make the Rhine, the Pyrennees and the Alps the frontiers of France. Again and again the French armies, led by brilliant generals, fought to gain lands to the north and east of France until the rest of Europe combined to stop French attacks. Louis' palace at Versailles was the sign of his wealth and power (see Plate 4). It was more than a palace: it was a town under one roof where the king, his nobles, courtiers, ministers and civil servants lived in great style. Everyone who came to it was impressed by the greatness of a country which could have so splendid a royal centre. And France was, indeed, a wealthy country. Her soil was rich and produced vast quantities of wheat, wine and cattle. The long rivers carried goods cheaply and her merchants and manufacturers were busy and skilful. At a time when coal and steam were not used in industry she was one of the leading manufacturing countries. This wealth permitted the king to keep a large army and navy.

* * *

Far away in the east of Europe a new country was being shaped and hammered into a Great Power. For a long time Russia had been a rather backward land, occupying the lands round Moscow but not stretching as far south as the Black Sea. To the west the Poles were enemies; the Baltic coast of modern Russia was then ruled by Sweden. North of the Black Sea the Turkish Empire ruled over the grassy plains, the steppes, of what is now southern Russia.

All this was changed by Peter the Great. He became Czar, or Emperor, in 1689 and at once gave himself the work of making Russia a modern country with seaports through which she could trade with the outside world. He himself went to England and Holland to learn how to do such things as build ships and make cannon, and he actually worked in the shipyards as a workman. When he returned he invited a great many foreigners to come out to Russia to teach his people Western ways of working. Among them were Scots fighting men. Soon after Peter

PETER THE GREAT, SHIPBUILDER

became Czar he appointed a new Commander-in-Chief of his armies: Patrick Gordon from Aberdeenshire, who had served in Russia for twenty years. Later, the Russian armies had another Scots general, Marshal James Keith, who came from a famous Scots family. Later still, Samuel Greig from Inverkeithing commanded the Russian fleet in the Mediterranean.

With the help of his foreign advisers Peter built up an army which was able to defeat the Swedes in a long war and take over some of the land ruled by Sweden on the Russian side of the Baltic. There, on the River Neva, he built his new capital which he named St. Petersburg; it is now called Leningrad. Notice what was happening. Before Peter's time the capital was Moscow, right in the heart of Russia and cut off from the West. Now it was a town built on a river flowing into the Baltic—a town in close touch with the lands of western Europe. For the next two hundred years Russia followed the ways of the countries of western Europe.

* * *

Today we think of Turkey as a small country, but in the seventeenth century it was a great empire ruling over all the lands on the south and east of the Mediterranean and stretching into Europe almost as far as Vienna. Indeed, it seemed at one time, in 1683, that the Turks would conquer Austria too. But after they had besieged Vienna for a long time they were defeated by an army under John Sobieski, a great Polish soldier who came to the help of the Austrians. After this defeat the Turks were, very slowly, driven down the valley of the River Danube by the Austrian emperors. By driving out the Turks the Austrians were able to make a great empire for themselves along the Danube.

* * *

In the north of Germany the little state of Brandenburg-Prussia was also being made stronger by its ruler, the

Great Elector, who ruled it from his capital at Berlin. We are more familiar with the country under the name of Prussia. In the next century Prussia, France, Russia and Austria were the most powerful countries of Europe.

THINGS TO DO

1. Write a paragraph on each of the following: The Holy Roman Empire; Gustavus Adolphus; Louis XIV; Peter the Great; John Sobieski.

2. Try to set down some of the reasons why so many Scotsmen should go abroad in the seventeenth century.

3. (*a*) From what you know of the geography of France make a list of the main crops grown there.

(*b*) What are the principal rivers of France, and what big towns are on those rivers?

4. What are the advantages and the drawbacks to Britain of being an island? Make a list of each.

7

Europeans in the New World

FROM the time when the Spaniards and Portuguese first discovered the new lands in the west and opened the sea-roads from Europe to India and America, men from western Europe began to settle in these lands. Where the countries were already civilised and full of people, the Europeans came in as traders and missionaries. In India and the East Indies the Portuguese were the first-comers. Later on, the Dutch drove them out of the East Indies, and Britain and France became the main powers in India. Where the newly-discovered lands belonged to people who were not highly civilised and who were few in number, the Europeans came as settlers and made a new Europe across the seas. In South and Central America many Spaniards and Portuguese settled, so that today Spanish is the language of all South America except Brazil, where Portuguese is spoken. In North America English is the language of all except the French Canadians. The West Indies, too, are peopled by the descendants of men from Europe and of the African slaves they brought in.

In this chapter we will see why Europeans left home to settle in North America, which parts they settled first, and how they managed to survive once they were there. It is important to know about this because many of these early

A RED INDIAN VILLAGE IN VIRGINIA

1 *Chief's house.* 2 *Place for prayer and images.*
3 *Ceremonial dance.* 4 *Feast.* 5 *Tobacco fields.* 6 *Watchman protecting maize.*
7 *Maize fields.* 8 *Pumpkin field.* 9 *Water supply.*

colonists came from Britain, and also because the U.S.A. and Canada are so important today. There is no time to study the settlement of South and Central America, but we should remember that long before the first Englishman set foot in North America, Spanish settlers were so plentiful in Mexico that a university had been set up in 1551.

The first English colony was Virginia, founded in 1607 by a London company. At first the people who went out were so busy trying to make their fortunes by finding gold that the colony almost starved. It was saved by two men —John Smith, an old soldier who had served in the Austrian army against the Turks, and John Rolfe. Smith brought some discipline into the colony and opposed the Indians. Rolfe taught the colonists that they could make their fortunes by hard work, by digging the ground and growing the Indian crop—tobacco. There was a great demand for tobacco in England and the colonists could sell all that they grew. Very soon Virginia became rich, and more men were encouraged to come out. Not all of these were Europeans. In 1619 the first ship-load of negro slaves was imported. John Rolfe has another claim to fame: he married Pocohantas, the daughter of an Indian king, Powhattan, and brought her to London where she was the wonder of the town.

The success of Virginia let men see that Englishmen could live well in America. Other colonies were soon set up. In 1620 some of the Puritans who had left England in the time of James VI and I and had gone to Holland, set sail from Plymouth to set up a new colony near Cape Cod on the New England shore, hoping that there they could worship God in their own way. Their little ship, the

Mayflower, left in September with 102 passengers, the 'Pilgrim Fathers'. In December they landed in a country that was almost deserted; for a plague of smallpox had recently killed off many of the Indians. The winter was very severe; food ran short and more than half the colonists were dead before summer came. But the rest carried on, helped by a friendly Indian who showed them how to grow Indian corn in little mounds with a decaying fish inside, and how to trap animals for fur and food. The first harvest was very important, for it meant the difference between plenty and starvation. The harvest was good and in the United States today Thanksgiving Day is still celebrated every year, to remind people of the thanksgiving for the first harvest.

From 1620 to 1640, when the Puritans were being harshly treated in England, thousands came out to join these Pilgrim Fathers. They settled mainly in Massachusetts, but some broke away and set up a new colony in Rhode Island. Generally all the area we call New England was settled by Puritans. To the south, Lord Baltimore set up the colony of Maryland for Roman Catholics. Another colony founded later for those who disagreed with the English government over religion was Pennsylvania, the colony started by William Penn for Quakers.

The map facing this page shows these early colonies.

Life for the first colonists was hard, especially in the north where there were no slaves to do the heavy work. The pioneer farmer had usually to clear the forest before he could make his fields, cutting down trees, digging up stumps and burning the wood. From some of the logs he had to build his wooden house and barns. Much of the furniture had to be hand made. For his wife the days were equally hard. She had bread to make, meat to salt for the long winter, wool to spin and skins to cure for clothing as well as all the other work which house-wives have everywhere. Life was made harder by the Indians. The settlers traded with them, exchanging rum, axes, knives and cloth for valuable furs, but they knew all the time that they

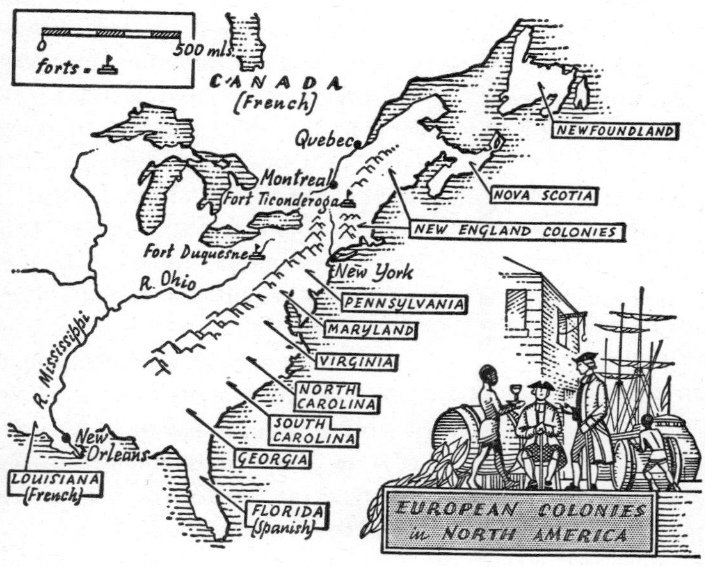

might hear the whooping war-cries of an Indian raid, or see their thatched houses set alight by Indian fire-arrows. In 1675 the Wampanoag Indians led an attack in which more than a thousand colonists were killed. The settlers lived with their guns beside them and became skilled backwoodsmen and marksmen, especially the Irish-Scots who settled in Pennsylvania. One of these fighting frontiersmen was Colonel Davy Crockett, who was born in Tennessee in 1786.

It was not only English colonists who moved into North America. The valley of the St. Lawrence was settled by French people, whose descendants still live there. Today in Canada one man in every four speaks French. Until 1666 these French colonists suffered from the attacks of the Iroquois, the best led and fiercest of the Indian nations. In that year the Iroquois were defeated and the way was open to the west. French fur-traders and missionaries pushed further and further into Canada, up the St. Lawrence and through the lakes in canoes and open boats. Others from the south settled along the Mississippi, creating the new state of Louisiana. This was a real danger to the English colonists, for if the French in Canada and the French in Louisiana joined up they would stop the English colonies from spreading westwards.

In all this great work of colonising, Scotland did little. Sir William Alexander of Menstrie bravely tried to set up a New Scotland, a Nova Scotia, in 1621. He was given a grant of Nova Scotia by King James and sent out two expeditions. Neither was a success. His son managed to start a small colony at Port Royal in the south of Nova Scotia, but Charles I in 1632 agreed to allow the French to take over Nova Scotia and the Scots colony came to an end. Many Scots, however, made their way to the English colonies and settled in New Jersey, Carolina and Pennsylvania. Along the frontier with the Indians many Scots from Ulster, Scots-Irish, settled and held the land.

Why did so many people leave Europe to start life afresh across the Atlantic? One answer we already know: Puritans, Catholics and Quakers came because they wanted to worship in their own ways. Others came in the hope of riches from discovering gold, from trading in furs, or from growing tobacco. Farmers came because land was dear in England and cheap in America. Some came unwillingly: African negroes were shipped as slaves, and many prisoners, both English and Scots, were transported to America.

The result of it all was that by 1700 nearly all the east coast of North America was held by Europeans, and others were pushing up the St. Lawrence and Mississippi valleys. The Red Indians were slowly being driven westwards and America was becoming a home for Europeans.

THINGS TO DO

1. Make a large map of North America. Mark on it the main rivers and lakes. Try to explain why these were so important in the early history of the colonists.

2. Make a scrap-book of American history to about 1700, including as many illustrations as possible.

3. Find out all you can about Davy Crockett.

4. Learn the names of the colonies shown on the map on page 57.

5. Write short notes on: The Pilgrim Fathers; John Rolfe; Nova Scotia; Thanksgiving Day.

6. Try to imagine that you are going to settle in New England in 1630. Make a list of all the necessary things you would have to take with you.

8

The Struggle between Britain and France

YOU will remember that in the fourteenth and fifteenth centuries there were long wars between England and France. These wars are called the Hundred Years War, and in them England was fighting to conquer France. In the eighteenth century there was a second and greater Hundred Years War between France and Britain, fought for a greater prize. This time they fought for control of the trade, the empty lands and the sea-roads of the world. Of course the fighting was not continuous, and there were long periods of peace, but we can say that for rather more than a hundred years the two countries were in opposite camps.

At first sight all the advantages seem to lie with France. In 1700 there were three or four times as many Frenchmen as there were Englishmen. Even when Scotland united with England, Britain did not contain nearly as many men as France. Then the French army was much larger and better organised than the British. The French navy was almost as large as Britain's, but Britain had one great advantage: she had no frontiers to guard. France had to keep up a vast army to guard her frontiers against Britain's allies; Britain could do with a small army and keep herself strong at sea, using her fleet to seize colonies and carry troops to fight in India and America.

Here is a list of the wars in which England and Britain fought against France in the second Hundred Years War:

War of the League of Augsburg	1689 to 1697
War of the Spanish Succession	1702 to 1713
War of the Austrian Succession	1740 to 1748
Seven Years War	1756 to 1763
War of American Independence	1775 to 1783
Revolutionary and Napoleonic Wars	1793 to 1815

During most of these wars British troops took no great part in the land-fighting in Europe. In the war of the Spanish Succession, however, under the Duke of Marlborough, the British army won many victories. Later, in the Napoleonic Wars, it drove the French out of Spain and, helped by the Prussians, defeated them finally at the Battle of Waterloo. Usually, however, we relied upon our allies to do the land-fighting in Europe while we fought at sea and in the colonies.

In these wars Britain gained much land oversea, especially in the Seven Years War. In fact, for Britain, this war lasted for almost nine years and gave us control of North America and India.

In North America the war began when the French tried to join their colonies in Canada and the Ohio Valley. As we saw in the last chapter, this was dangerous, for the English colonists and fur traders from Virginia were already moving into this area between Lake Erie and the tributaries of the Ohio. When the French built a fort,

Fort Duquesne, where Pittsburgh now stands, Virginia sent some soldiers under a young colonel called George Washington to drive them out. Washington and his men were taken prisoner. This was serious, and in 1755 the British government sent a regular soldier, General Braddock, with regular troops to drive out the French. The red-coated soldiers, with fifes shrilling at the head of the column, made their way slowly westwards towards Fort Duquesne. But all the way they were shadowed by silent redmen who knew how to remain unseen in the woods. Just before Braddock reached Fort Duquesne the Indians and their French masters struck. Two-thirds of the British force were killed or wounded, including General Braddock. Fair-haired scalps hung in the wigwams afterwards.

The next two years were difficult years in North America. Until William Pitt became Prime Minister in 1757 things went badly for Britain. They might have been worse but for

Sir William Johnson, the king's agent for Indian affairs, who had a wonderful gift for dealing with Indians and managed to keep both the Mohawks and the Iroquois friendly.

Pitt's leadership changed everything. We should remember that it was Pitt who encouraged Highlanders to join the British army. In North America these Highland soldiers distinguished themselves first at the attack on a French fort, Ticonderoga, and then at Quebec. The year 1759 was the wonderful year when victory followed victory in Europe, at sea, in India and in North America.

In North America Quebec, the key to Canada, was taken. The way was prepared by James Cook, later to be famous as an explorer, who did much of the charting of the river leading to the city while the troops were preparing for their task. In September a small force of British troops under General Wolfe landed below the steep cliff which rises from the St. Lawrence at Quebec. In darkness they climbed silently up to the Plains of Abraham. A French sentry challenged: a highland officer answered in French, and then silenced him. By morning the whole British force was in position and by evening the French were defeated. In the battle both commanders were killed, Wolfe and Montcalm. General Wolfe was an officer of great courage and skill and, moreover, a man of kindness:

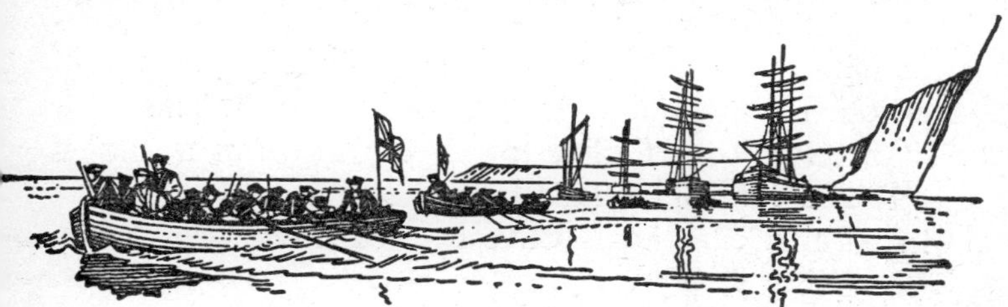

SCALING THE HEIGHTS OF ABRAHAM

after Culloden he had almost ruined his career by refusing to kill wounded highlanders.

After Quebec had fallen the way up the St. Lawrence was open. Other British forces had taken Fort Duquesne and were advancing towards the Great Lakes. When peace came France was glad to surrender all her lands in North America. In this one war Britain gained Canada and all the rest of North America as far west as the Mississippi, for we had also taken Florida from Spain, the ally of France.

Meanwhile, on the other side of the world, in India, Britain was equally successful. There was great confusion there. In 1707 the Mogul Empire really came to an end and the various princes of India were warring among themselves. Each prince hoped that with the help of European weapons and soldiers he would be able to defeat his rivals. On the other hand, the French and British trading companies hoped that with the help of Indian princes they would be able to increase their wealth and power. As a result, both Britain and France found allies among the princes. At first things favoured the French. The French governor of Pondicherry, Dupleix, was a brave, determined man who was resolved that south India should be French. In the War of the Austrian Succession the French captured Madras but were forced to hand it back when war ended. Even after the peace treaty, however, fighting continued between the princes, and both French and British troops took part. This gave a chance for Robert Clive to prove his skill as a soldier and to win control of India from the French.

In his first campaigns Clive showed his genius with a

very small force—six officers, two hundred British and three hundred Indian soldiers. He captured the great town of Arcot and held it against ten thousand enemy troops for fifty days in spite of fierce attacks on the gates by armour-plated elephants. As a result of his victory a

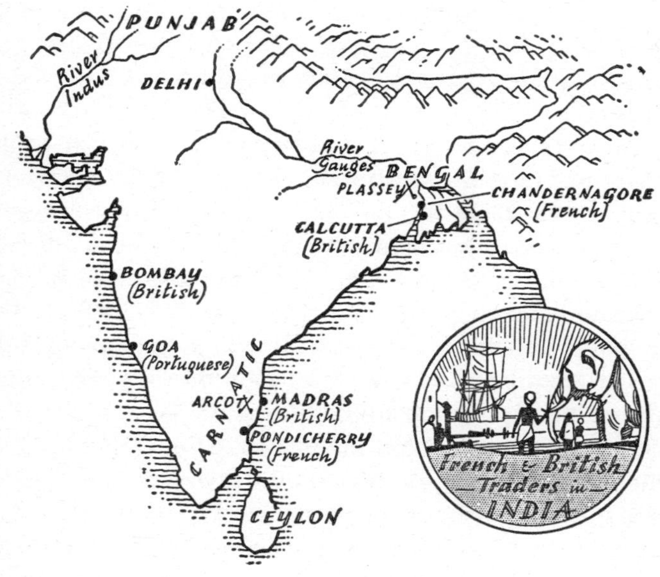

prince who was a friend of Britain was made ruler of the south-east of India, the Carnatic.

Further north, at Calcutta, Clive had to act to save what remained of the British trading-post there. In 1756 the ruler of Bengal, Suraj-ud-daula, had imprisoned 146 of the British in a small, overcrowded cell; and during the night all except twenty-three died. This was the 'Black

Hole of Calcutta'. To avenge this, Clive was sent north with an army of about three thousand men, of whom some nine hundred were British. He recaptured Calcutta and fought Suraj-ud-daula's forces at Plassey in 1757. It was an outstanding victory over very great odds, for Suraj-ud-daula had nearly fifty thousand men. After the battle Clive appointed as ruler of Bengal a prince who was friendly to Britain.

One more step was needed to weaken French power, for in the Deccan, the great plateau of south India, the French were still strong. From Bengal a small force was sent to capture Masulipatam and its French garrison. Once it was in British hands the ruler of the Deccan hurried to become an ally of Britain. By 1763 French power in India was broken, and the British merchants had the trade between India and Europe in their own hands. We should remember the words 'British merchants'. For it was the great East India Company, 'John Company', and not the British government, that ruled India. Gradually the Company came more and more under the control of the British government, but its rule did not finally end until 1858.

We have said nothing about the war in Europe, and instead we have looked closely at America and India, because in the long run Britain's wealth and power depended on her lands beyond the seas. The Indian trade made work for many people in this country: for example, Indian jute made a great industry in Dundee. To North America hundreds of thousands of people have gone from Britain, and especially from Scotland to Canada, to find new homes in a richer land. Today India and Canada are two of our great partners in the Commonwealth of Nations.

THINGS TO DO

1. Find out as much as you can about the men mentioned in this chapter: William Pitt, General Wolfe, Captain Cook, Robert Clive.

2. Write short notes on (*a*) The importance of the capture of Quebec; (*b*) The 'Black Hole of Calcutta'; (*c*) The battle of Plassey.

3. Collect pictures of soldiers of this time and see what you can learn about their uniforms and weapons.

4. In the chapter you have just read we have mentioned the importance of jute to Scotland. Make a list of the other main imports to Britain from India.

9

The U.S.A. is Born

THE Seven Years War left Britain as the strongest power in North America; she owned a great belt of land stretching the whole way down the eastern coast, from Hudson's Bay to Florida. It seemed that all was well, but in fact the driving out of the French weakened Britain. Up till now the colonists had realised that they needed British soldiers and British ships to protect them from the French. When the French were driven out British forces no longer seemed necessary, and the colonists resented very much having to pay a share of the cost of defence, especially when they were not represented in Parliament. We shall see that twenty years after the Peace of Paris, Britain lost the original thirteen colonies in North America.

The trouble began almost at once. An Indian chief, Pontiac, raised a rebellion against the white settlers—the greatest Indian rising there ever was. His men killed many settlers around the Great Lakes and burned many of the log forts and stockades before they were finally defeated. One reason for the rising had been that the Indians feared that they would lose their lands to the white settlers. To prevent further trouble the British government ordered settlers not to cross the Appalachian Mountains until treaties were made with the Indians. To the men in the colonies this seemed to be nonsense; for them the land to the west was the Land of Promise: rich, fertile land from which the French had been driven. It seemed to them that the British government was deliberately favouring the Indians. So they ignored the Proclamation Line, as the boundary was called, moved west down the great Ohio River, and defied the government in London and the British soldiers in the forts beyond the mountains.

To raise the money needed to pay for the soldiers in North America the London government tried to increase the amount of money which they received from the colonists. There were two main ways of doing this: by customs, the taxes paid on goods coming into a country; and by excise, the taxes paid on goods made or sold inside the country. The customs officers were never popular. Even during the war with France, when they tried to stop American merchants trading with the enemy, they were hated, for the colonists loathed the laws which hindered their trade. In 1764 Parliament at Westminster put heavy customs duties on such foreign goods as silk, sugar and wine. This Act, the Sugar Act, was very unpopular. In the following year the Stamp Act was passed, and this was still more unpopular. It laid down that all legal documents, newspapers, advertisements, playing cards, and so on, had to be stamped before they were sold. This excise duty affected a great many people and there was such an outcry that the Act was repealed in 1766. But the damage was done. The colonists saw that the British Parliament meant to tax them, although the colonies were not represented in Parliament.

Open trouble began in 1770 in Boston when a crowd of

rowdies surrounded a patrol of British troops, throwing stones and jeering at the soldiers. The troops opened fire and killed a few of the mob. The colonists called this 'The Boston Massacre'. A few years later Boston was the centre of more trouble. Until 1773 it had been hard to sell tea from British India in the colonies because tea smuggled from Holland was cheaper. The Tea Act of 1773 reduced the price of British tea so much that it sold cheaper than Dutch tea. But there was still a tax on the British tea, and many people in the colonies thought that the price had been reduced simply to make them pay the tax. A band of colonists disguised as Red Indians boarded a tea-ship in Boston harbour and threw the tea overboard. All up and down the coast others followed their example. It was open rebellion, and the 'Boston Tea Party' is usually thought of as the beginning of the break-away from Britain.

The war began with a little skirmish. In April 1775 the British governor of Boston, General Gage, sent a force of troops to seize a gunpowder magazine at Concord. During the night Paul Revere and William Dawes, two men of Boston, rode out to warn the 'minutemen', colonists who said they were ready to march at a minute's notice to resist the British. So when the British forces arrived at a little village called Lexington fifty 'minutemen' tried to stop them. This little battle began a war which lasted for eight years and ended with the defeat of the British and the setting up of the United States.

In 1776 the leaders of the colonists met and signed a statement of their beliefs that 'all men are born free and equal' and declared that the colonies were independent of

Britain. This document is called the Declaration of Independence, and you will find part of it on page 75. The Americans still keep the day on which it was signed, July 4th, as 'Independence Day'.

In the actual fighting neither side did well. The well-

THE 'BOSTON TEA PARTY'

drilled, red-coated British soldiers (and the German regiments which King George III hired to help them) were rather at a loss to know how to deal with the Americans who fired from behind trees and were very difficult to catch. The colonial forces were often short of powder, of shoes, even of food. They had one great advantage: in George Washington they had a great leader, a man who was absolutely unshakable. Later he became the first President of the United States, but his greatest work was done during the war when he kept together his poorly-equipped colonial soldiers and led them to victory. At first neither side could claim any definite victory, but in October 1777 the colonists had their first success. At

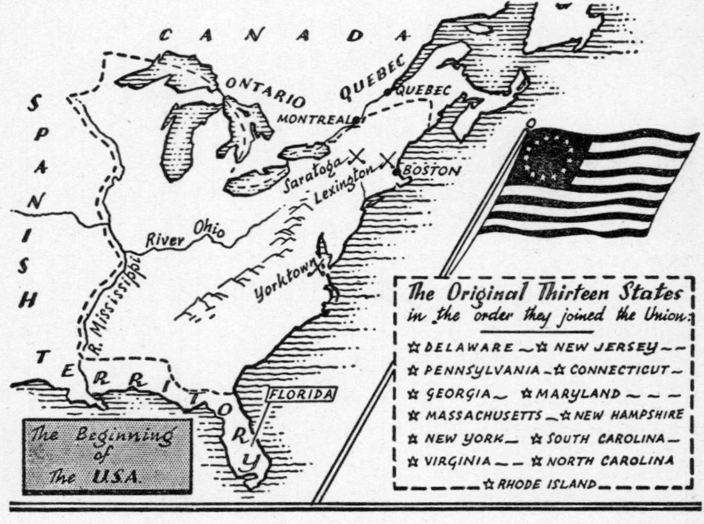

Saratoga General Burgoyne and his army of 4,500 men had to surrender.

The victory was a very important one. Up till now other European countries had been watching the war, expecting the British to win. Now they realised that the colonists had a chance. France and Spain came into the war against Britain and we had to fight on sea as well as on land, in Europe as well as in America. For example, the Spanish besieged Gibraltar, French troops landed in America, and a great sea battle—the Battle of the Saints—was fought between the British and French fleets in the West Indies. The colonists, too, were creating a navy. Paul Jones, the son of a Scots gardener from Kirkcudbright, was one of its founders and was one of the first to fly the 'stars and stripes' in a ship of war. In his ship the *Bonhomme Richard*, he raided the British coast and even defeated a frigate, the *Serapis*.

By 1782 Britain was ready to think of peace. Another British army had been forced to surrender at Yorktown and the war was becoming very expensive and very unpopular. In 1783 the Peace of Versailles ended the war and left the colonists free of British rule, free to form their own country—the United States of America.

Of course not everyone in the colonies had rebelled against Britain. Many had remained loyal, including such people as Flora MacDonald and most of the highlanders who had gone to settle in the Carolinas. After the war was over many of these loyalists left the United States to settle in Canada, in Ontario and New Brunswick. During the war the people of Canada had remained loyal to Britain, for the French Catholics thought that life would be better for them under British rule than under the rule of the Puritans of New England. The arrival of the new settlers in Ontario and New Brunswick meant that Canada now had a large number of English-speaking settlers. So one result of the British defeat in America was that Canada began to grow into an English-speaking colony.

When the people of the United States began to think how they should govern themselves, they gave up the idea of having a new king to replace George III. Instead they set up a republic and elected George Washington as President. In place of Parliament they set up Congress: this, like Parliament, has two houses. One is called the House of Representatives and corresponds to our House of Commons; the other is called the Senate, in which there are two representatives from every state, large and small. Congress, like Parliament, makes laws for the whole country. In addition, each state has the right to make laws which apply to its own members only.

This young country grew very quickly. Settlers pushed westwards into the new lands till they reached the Pacific Ocean. When the War of Independence started there were fewer than two million people in the colonies. Today the population of the United States is over 150 millions and the United States is one of the two greatest Powers in the world.

THINGS TO DO

1. Begin a scrap-book of the history of the United States. Collect all the information you can from newspapers, magazines, and so on. Arrange them and paste them in a notebook.

2. Imagine that you are a colonist living in Boston in 1774. Write a letter to a friend explaining why you dislike British rule.

3. Find out as much as you can about George Washington. Write a short life-story or prepare a talk on him to give to the class.

4. Read carefully this part of the Declaration of Independence. Try to understand what it means, and copy all, or part, of it in your notebook:

'We hold these truths to be self-evident, that all men are created equal, that they are endowed by their Creator with certain unalienable rights, that among these are life, liberty and the pursuit of happiness. . . . Whenever any form of government becomes destructive of these ends, it is the right of the people to alter or to abolish it, and to institute a new government . . . as shall seem most likely to effect their safety and happiness.'

10

The French Revolution and Napoleon

A THRILL of excitement ran through Europe in 1789: the French parliament, the States-General, which had not met for more than one hundred and fifty years, was called together. To us there is nothing very thrilling in the idea of the meeting of a parliament, but in 1789 almost every country in Europe, except Britain, was ruled by a king without any parliament. No one could be sure where this change in France would lead to. The king, Louis XVI, was not particularly eager to call it, but his hand was forced. France was almost bankrupt; taxes were appallingly heavy; many of the people were desperately poor. To find money the king had to have a parliament.

When it met, it took charge and began to put right many of the things which were wrong in France: the power of the nobles was taken away, taxes were spread more evenly, laws were reformed, and so on. In all this there was nothing to worry about. The trouble came from the people, the labouring people both in Paris and in the country, who thought that the States-General were not going fast enough. In Paris, on July 14th, a mob seized the royal fortress-prison, the Bastille, killed the guards and captured arms. In the country many of the peasants attacked the nobles' castles, burnt them and took the land.

Some of these nobles fled to foreign countries and took with them stories of what was happening in France. Men realised that this was revolution, especially when a crowd of hungry people from Paris marched to the royal palace at Versailles and forced the king and his family to return to Paris.

THE STORMING OF THE BASTILLE

At first the States-General had hoped to give France a government rather like that of Great Britain, where the king ruled with the help and advice of parliament, but obviously that would succeed only if the king agreed. In 1792 Louis and his family tried to flee from France. He was arrested and tried. The sentence was death both for himself and for the queen, the hated Marie Antoinette:

death by the guillotine, a machine for cutting off heads cleanly. He did not die alone, for a very large number of nobles were also tried and executed. The heavy carts carried them from prison to the public squares in Paris and other towns where the tall guillotines were set up and the crowds gloated over the deaths of the aristocrats. It was the Reign of Terror.

We must not think of the French Revolution simply as a time when nobles were killed. Many great reforms were made which have lasted till today. The watchwords were 'Liberty, Equality and Fraternity', and these ideas are the basis of what we mean by democracy today. All the laws which prevented men from being free and equal were repealed. Even the systems of measurement were changed and the metric system which we use in science was brought in.

Outside France men watched carefully what was happening. To some it was the greatest event they had ever known. They saw that the changes in France might be an example to their own countries. In the summer of 1792 in many Scottish towns crowds demonstrated against the government and in the highlands soldiers had to be called in to stop the crofters driving away the great herds of sheep which the lairds brought in. The government replied by bringing some of the leaders to trial. Thomas Muir and Thomas Palmer were both sentenced to be transported to Australia and two other leaders were hanged. But the sympathy with the French revolutionaries continued until Britain and France came to war.

This long war, which lasted from 1793 to 1815, began when the French revolutionaries declared war on Austria, hoping to spread the ideas of the revolution all over Europe. The French army seemed to be in bad shape, but although many of the officer-nobles had left, the newly appointed officers and the soldiers had something that made up for their lack of skill. They believed passionately in France and in the revolution. The stirring words and music of the *Marseillaise*, which was written at this time, gives us some idea of the spirit of France. In a short campaign the Austrians and Prussians were expelled from France. Belgium was conquered, then Holland. A small British army which landed in Holland under the Duke of York was defeated and forced to retreat through Emden. Everywhere France was victorious at first. Soon she was to be served by the greatest soldier of his age.

Napoleon Bonaparte, a Corsican, had been an artillery officer of the royal army in France. When the revolution came he stayed on and made a name for himself by helping to drive a British force out of Toulon. His great chance came when he was given command of the army of Italy. In 1796 he began to conquer Italy, which was then a collection of small independent states. By 1797 the campaign was over: Italy was conquered and large parts of it made into republics like France. Austria and Prussia had made peace and Britain alone remained at war with France.

The next year Napoleon tried to knock Britain out of the war by an attack, through Egypt, on our trade in the Indian Ocean. He succeeded in landing a great army in Egypt and defeating the Egyptians, but a British fleet under Horatio Nelson caught his ships in Aboukir Bay at the mouth of the Nile, destroyed them and so cut off the French army. In France men did not understand how serious this naval defeat was, for they thought of Napoleon simply as a great hero who had conquered Egypt. When he came back to France he was welcomed everywhere and made head of the government, with the title of First Consul. By 1802 both France and Britain realised that neither had much hope of victory: it was a war of elephant against whale. The Peace of Amiens ended this first stage of the war.

After a short-lived peace, war broke out again in 1804. France and Spain fought on one side; Britain, Russia, Austria (and later Prussia) on the other. Napoleon's first plan was to invade Britain, by carrying a large army over the English Channel in rafts and flat-bottomed landing-craft. A great army was assembled on the French coast and exercised in embarking and disembarking. In Britain great preparations were made to meet the invasion: men were enlisted in the Fencibles and Militia—the 'Home Guard' of the time; bonfires were built on high ground to be lit if the enemy landed; above all, the Navy was ordered to seek out and destroy the French fleet. The Navy succeeded in its task. On October 21st, 1805, Lord Nelson shattered the combined French and Spanish fleets at Trafalgar, to give Britain the mastery of the seas for the next hundred years.

Even before that great victory, Napoleon had been forced to withdraw his troops from the Channel and hurry eastwards, for Russia and Austria had mobilised against him. In this campaign Europe was shown how great a soldier Napoleon was. At Austerlitz in 1805 the Austrian army was defeated; at Jena in 1806 the Prussian army was defeated; and finally after a long march across Poland,

Napoleon forced the Russians to make peace at Tilsit. All Europe was subdued, except for Britain. Against Britain Napoleon tried a new weapon—blockade. The countries of Europe were forbidden to trade with Britain. The weapon was two-edged: it caused unemployment in Britain, but it stirred up much ill-feeling against Napoleon in Europe, where men needed British goods.

Indeed, it led to a renewal of the land-fighting. Portugal refused to obey, and when French troops invaded Portugal, Britain was able to send troops to fight the French there and in Spain. This war, which we call the Peninsular War, did not end till the British, commanded by the Duke of Wellington, had driven the French from Spain and had occupied the south of France. In the east, too, Napoleon's blockade caused trouble. The Czar of Russia disliked it very much, for it prevented British manufactured goods from reaching Russia. Finally he decided to pay no attention to Napoleon's wishes. Once more Napoleon led a great army eastwards, this time to disaster. In 1812 he crossed the Russian frontier at the head of his men. Slowly the French made their way across the great Russian plain, defeating the Russians at Borodino. Moscow was captured, but Russia was not defeated. As Napoleon's forces marched back into Europe, they were attacked repeatedly by Russian cavalry. Winter came on early, and the bitter cold of Russia killed thousands of men: only a fragment of the great army came back into Europe.

That was the beginning of Napoleon's downfall. In 1813 the Austrians, Russians and Prussians combined to beat him at Leipzig in the 'Battle of the Nations'. France was invaded, and in the end Napoleon gave up the throne

of France and went into exile on Elba. Europe seemed to be at peace again.

In 1815 another storm burst upon Europe: Napoleon came back from Elba. His soldiers came flocking back to join him and serve under the red, white and blue flag. At Waterloo in Belgium the last battle of the war was fought. All day long the red-coated British troops under the Duke of Wellington held the fierce French attacks. As evening came on, the Prussians under Blücher came to help, and

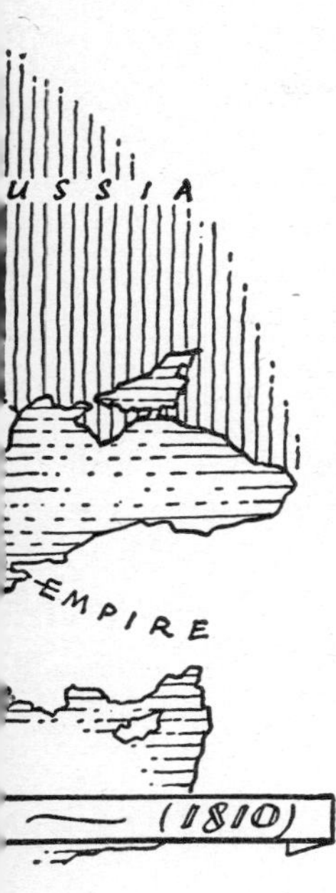

the French were finally defeated. Napoleon was sent to St. Helena (where he died in 1821); and Paris was occupied by the allies. Not all Napoleon's work ended in 1815. The great work he did to reform French law survived and France to-day lives under the Napoleonic law code. In addition, the glory of Napoleon's conquests lived on in Frenchmen's memories. Years after his death, his body was brought back to Paris to be re-buried in the magnificent tomb where it now lies.

In the long wars Scotsmen of all ranks had played a great part, none greater than that of Sir John Moore. We remember him as the commander who reformed part of the Army and made that part a model to the rest. In the war in Spain we began to use light infantry, soldiers armed with the newly invented rifle and trained to move quickly and fight in small groups. Sir John saw that these troops would be useless unless they were encouraged to think for themselves and act for themselves. His new methods of training made the light infantry very efficient. This, too, was the time when many famous Highland regiments were added to the British army—the 79th, Cameron Highlanders, the 92nd, Gordon Highlanders, the 91st and 93rd, Argyll and Sutherland Highlanders, as well as others now disbanded. At sea the greatest Scots admiral was Admiral Duncan, who won a great victory over the Dutch fleet in 1797 at Camperdown.

At home the war had meant prosperity for many. Farming was very profitable because food was scarce. The iron workers (and therefore the coal miners) had plenty of work to supply the weapons needed for Britain and her allies. Carron in particular was very busy making the famous guns, the carronades, which were very much used at this time. Sail-makers, too, were very busy. On the other hand, we must remember that Napoleon's blockade kept our goods out of many European countries and that there was, as a result, a good deal of unemployment as the war went on. We should remember as well that food was dear. Many went hungry both in the Highlands, where sheep-farming was spreading, and in the manufacturing towns of the Lowlands.

We began by saying that the rulers of Europe were shocked in 1789. They suffered many more shocks before 1815, and when Napoleon was defeated they resolved never again to allow France to become a danger to Europe. For a long time the Great Powers tried to put down any attempts to give ordinary people any say in the running of any country. Countries such as Italy and Germany, which had been partly unified under Napoleon, were broken up again into many small states. The Great Powers made themselves greater by taking over more land. Thus Great Britain kept Malta, Ceylon, and the Cape of Good Hope; Austria took the north of Italy; Prussia took most of Saxony; and Russia added Poland to her great lands. In France, King Louis XVIII, the brother of Louis XVI, was put on the throne. No one paid any attention to the wishes of the people, unfortunately. The rulers thought that the danger from France had ended when Napoleon was defeated: they did not understand that the ideas of the French Revolution—Liberty, Equality and Fraternity—were more dangerous to them than even the French armies.

THINGS TO DO

1. Write short notes on: The Reign of Terror; Thomas Muir; Battle of Aboukir Bay; Trafalgar; The Retreat from Moscow; Waterloo.

2. See if you can learn and sing the *Marseillaise* in French or English.

3. From what you have learned in your science lessons write down the main units of measurement in the metric system. Try to explain why this system is such a very good one.

4. Explain clearly in your own words why there was a revolution in France.

5. Make a time-chart of events from 1789 to 1815.

6. Try to borrow from the library some of the books of Baroness Orczy about the 'Scarlet Pimpernel'; and some of those by C. S. Forester about the naval war—*Mr. Midshipman Hornblower* and others.

II

Kings, Queens and Cabinets

So far we have said very little about Parliament and the government of the country and we have not learned lists of kings, queens and dates. It is, however, sometimes very useful to know which king or queen was ruling at any particular time. Until fairly recently kings and queens had a great deal to do with running the country, and we can often see that certain things happened because the king decided that they should. Besides, knowing the reigns of different kings is sometimes a useful way of breaking up time into smaller stretches which you can remember more easily.

All the rulers of Britain since 1603 are descended from the Scottish kings, from James VI and his ancestors, since Elizabeth of England had no children. Until 1714 our rulers were descended from James VI's son Charles I; after 1714 they are the descendants of James's daughter Elizabeth, who married the German Elector Palatine. A list of rulers and the dates of their reigns appear opposite.

Refer to this list as you read later chapters, and see from it which sovereign was reigning in Britain at the time of the important happenings you read about.

Since the Union of the Crowns in 1603 the king's power has grown less and the power of Parliament has grown

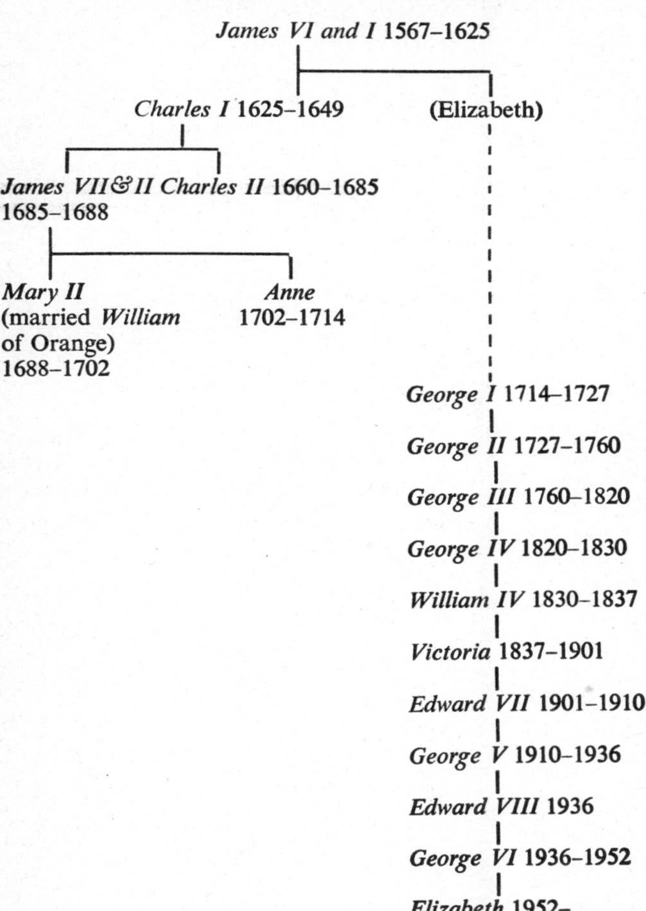

very much greater. The king's power was weakened during the Civil War, when the English Parliament claimed many rights. It was weakened still more in 1688–1689 at the revolution which drove out James VII. When George I became king he could speak little English and had to rely very much on his English-speaking ministers to rule for him.

Notice this word 'minister'. We use it to describe both clergymen and the heads of government departments. We speak of 'ministers of religion' and of the 'Prime Minister'. The word meant 'servant' originally. The parish minister is the servant of his parish, and the Prime Minister was the king's chief servant. To begin with, the king could appoint as his 'servants' or ministers any men he wished, and he did not have to follow their advice if he did not like it. Under the first three Georges this slowly changed, and most of the king's ministers were chosen from members of Parliament. (Even today, remember, members of the government need not be members of Parliament though they almost always are.) The ministers met together to talk over what they should do, and this committee of ministers was called a 'cabinet'. One of them was recognised as the leader and spokesman—the prime minister—although he was not called that at first.

In the reign of Charles II there grew up groups or 'parties' of people who wanted to govern the country in different ways. The first parties were nicknamed Whigs and Tories, and these nicknames lasted until Queen Victoria's reign. Obviously a 'cabinet' will work best if its members agree about most things. So it became the custom to choose members of a cabinet from one party, the party which had most members in the House of Commons.

This change to a government by a prime minister and cabinet was helped by the wisdom and skill of great statesmen. In the reign of George I Sir Robert Walpole kept Britain at peace for nearly twenty years and became so important in governing the country that we can really think of him as the first Prime Minister. Later the two Pitts, William Earl of Chatham, and his son William after him, proved themselves to be great leaders who carried the country through the Seven Years War and the wars against Napoleon. In the reign of Queen Victoria the two great Prime Ministers were Disraeli and Gladstone. By their time the names of the parties had changed. Disraeli was the leader of the Conservative party which had grown out of the old Tory party. Gladstone was the leader of the Liberal party which had grown out of the Whigs. In this century the Liberal party has become a very small one and we now have a Labour party and a Conservative party as the two main groups. The last of the great Liberal Prime Ministers was Lloyd George, who led the country through the first world war.

We will not read much more just now about changes in government, for in the next part of this book we are going to find out as much as we can about the life and work of the people of Britain. For the moment, then, we should remember that in the years between James VI and ourselves the power of kings has lessened. In its place we have a way of government in which a prime minister and a cabinet of ministers rule the country. These men are responsible to Parliament for what they do, and our Parliament is elected by the people of Britain.

THINGS TO DO

1. Explain carefully the following words: a 'party' (such as the Labour party and the Conservative party); 'cabinet'; 'minister'.

2. Write one sentence on each of the following great statesmen who were Prime Ministers: Walpole; the Elder Pitt and the Younger Pitt; Disraeli; Gladstone; Lloyd George.

Part Two

LIFE AND WORK

12

Work in the Country

YOU will remember that we 'visited' the Scottish lowlands at the time of Alexander III. Then we had another look at the countryside in the reign of Mary Stuart, three hundred years later, and we saw that ways of farming had not changed very much. What is even more surprising, by the time of the Union of the Parliaments in 1707 Scots folk still farmed their land as their forefathers had done for centuries.

Much of the land was bare hill, rough moorland or squelchy marsh. The marshy land was really the best, but as it had not yet been drained the higher land was ploughed for growing crops. This ploughed land still lay in unfenced patches as had been the custom for hundreds of years. The infield was given most attention and was cropped every year without a rest. The outfield patches were ploughed for a few years and then rested—but manured very seldom. Folk believed that

> If land be three years out and three years in
> It will keep in good heart till the de'il grows blin'.

The infield and outfield were still divided into ridges or 'rigs' which changed hands every year. Each man looked after his own rigs, but at ploughing, sowing and harvest they all worked together. The old heavy wooden ploughs were still in use, 'more fit to raise laughter than raise soil', one Scots lord said.

The same crops were still grown: oats, barley, some wheat, and, in some districts, flax for linen. The seed was so poor that often they reaped only three ears for each one sown. Then they had 'ane to saw, ane to gnaw, and ane to pay the laird witha'—because rents were still paid in food and service and not in money. The cattle and sheep were small and scraggy. A large number of them were killed in the autumn and the others fed on hay in their owners' houses until the spring 'lifting time'.

The houses of the ordinary folk were built much as they had been for centuries: stone walls, heather-thatch roofs, no glass windows to let the light in or proper chimneys to let the peat reek out. We would think them terribly dirty but, they used to say, 'the clartier the cosier'.

Their clothes, too, were very simple. The women wore

dresses of undyed woollen cloth spun at home. The men wore rough shirts of wool or a coarse linen called 'harn', and cloth breeches. On Sundays they dressed for the kirk in their best clothes and painfully put on shoes and stockings. The women wore a kind of headscarf of harn, called

COUNTRY FOLK ABOUT 1700

a 'toy', and a coloured plaid over head and shoulders. The men wore suits of homespun cloth and blue bonnets.

Everything for their meals, Sunday and weekday alike, was provided by their land or their beasts. They had porridge, broth made with kail, peas and beans, bannocks and oatcakes with milk and ale. They did not eat much meat, but sometimes salmon from the nearby river or herring if they were near the sea, or salted fish.

In most years, then, Scotland's soil, rivers and sea provided enough for her folk to live in their simple way. But years of bad harvests were years of tragedy. Just before 1700 there were seven bad harvests in a row. Then, we are told, a fifth of the population became beggars. There were other famines in later years, but during the eighteenth century there came great changes in ways of farming. After these changes, more and better food was produced.

About 1725 several landowners saw that the old ways were wasteful and they formed a 'Society for Improving in the Knowledge of Agriculture'. Such men were called 'Improvers'. Some of them were lairds, such as Sir Archibald Grant of Monymusk in Aberdeenshire and Adam Cockburn of Ormiston in East Lothian. Some were nobles such as the Earl of Haddington and the Duke of Atholl. Men like these brought in ideas from England and Holland.

In England, Robert Bakewell had shown how bigger and better cattle could be bred. Jethro Tull had invented a seed drill which saved seed by sowing it in straight rows, thus making weeding easier. Lord Townshend had lived in Holland and discovered what a useful crop turnips were. Like clover, they provided winter feed for cattle and gave the land a rest from growing oats, barley and wheat.

Other lessons were learned too. Marshes were drained.

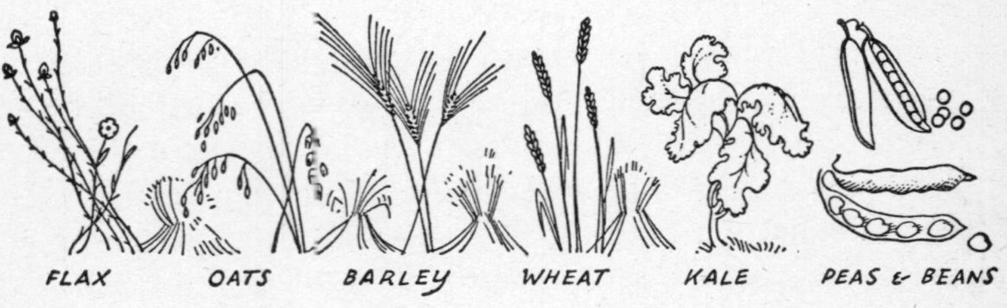

Trees were planted to protect crops as well as to provide timber. Farmers discovered the usefulness of lime to keep the soil sweet and of ground bones to fertilise it. New machines came into use. From Holland James Meikle of Saltoun brought the idea of a mill for grinding grain. James's son, Andrew, who lived in Dunbar, invented a threshing machine to take the place of the old flails. Later, after 1800, the minister of Carmyllie, Patrick Bell, invented the first reaping machine.

These changes and new ideas did not catch on easily. To begin with, men were suspicious of queer crops and queer machines. Secondly, a man could not use new methods if his land was split up in different rigs and if it changed hands each year. So men began to 'enclose' the land with dykes or hedges, and the fields so formed were rented for a number of years. This was much better for the men who wanted to use the new methods, and soon after 1800 the runrig way of farming had disappeared in most of Scotland.

In these 'enclosed' farms, better crops and better animals were produced. On the fertile soils of the Lothians and the East Neuk of Fife, for example, farmers now grow heavy crops of wheat, oats and barley, as well as potatoes, hay and turnips. In the rich pastures of Ayrshire they are mainly interested in dairy farming. The Ayrshire and

Galloway breeds of cattle are famous. In the north-east, bullocks are bred for beef and Aberdeen Angus cattle are among the best beef animals in the world. Lanarkshire horses, the Clydesdale breed, were very popular before the days of the tractor. Other parts of Scotland specialise too. The Borders and the Shetlands produce high-quality wool. Growers in Arran and on the Ayrshire coast improved their potato crops and they are now grown in most districts in Scotland. In fact, 'Scotch' seed potatoes are sent in large quantities to English growers. Soft fruit and vegetables are grown on a large scale in the Clyde Valley and the Carse of Gowrie; Carluke and Dundee have large jam factories because they are in these districts.

But in the Highlands enclosures brought unhappiness. There the land was enclosed for sheep farms and often the landowners' factors made brutal 'clearances'. Men, women and children were turned out of their houses: 15,000 of them in the years between 1800 and 1805. Some of them went to the towns and found work in the new factories. Many emigrated to Canada, America and Australia. Today folk are still drifting away from the highland glens to the towns, though for different reasons.

So the changes in the countryside from 1707 to the present day have brought difficulties as well. We have more and better food, and people live more comfortably. Scotland as a whole is richer, but our Highlands are poorer. Try to find out what is being done to make them richer too.

THINGS TO DO

1. Explain the following:

   (*a*) 'If land be three years out and three years in
   It will keep in good heart till the de'il grows blin'.'

   (*b*) 'Ane to saw, ane to gnaw,
   And ane to pay the laird witha'.'

   (*c*) 'Lifting time.'

2. Make sure you know the meanings of: infield, outfield, rigs, runrig, harn, toy, enclosed land.

3. Write a sentence about each of these men to show how their work was important: The 'Improvers', Robert Bakewell, Jethro Tull, Lord Townshend, James Meikle, Andrew Meikle, Patrick Bell.

4. What were the results of the enclosures in lowland and highland Scotland? Write a paragraph on

   'Farming in lowland Scotland today' and
   'The Highland Clearances'.

Pay particular attention to your own district or other districts you know well.

13

Work in the Towns

LOOK at the diagram on this page. It shows two very strange things. First, the population of Scotland has grown from about one and a quarter million people in 1700 to over five million today. Next, look where most people lived in 1700: four out of every five were farmers and country-dwellers. Today five out of every six of us live in towns. To

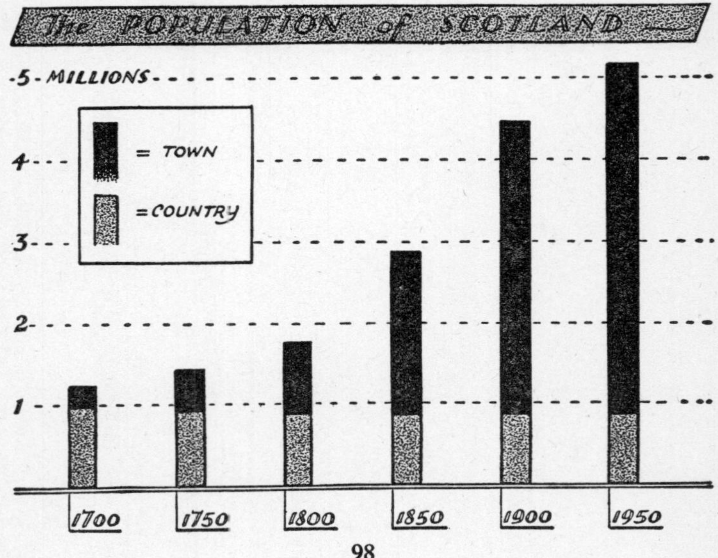

put it in another way, the number of country folk today is about the same as it was in 1700—but there are twenty times as many people living in towns. Look how Glasgow and Edinburgh have grown, for example.

Obviously there must be much more work in towns than there used to be—especially in the south-west of Scotland. Goods that used to be made in the countryside on a small scale are now manufactured in town factories. In the early eighteenth century many people earned their living in linen-making and the tobacco trade. Later, cotton-making and the iron and steel industries became much more important. These big changes in industries we call the 'Industrial Revolution'; and the biggest changes took place in Scotland between 1770 and 1850. Let us see how it all happened.

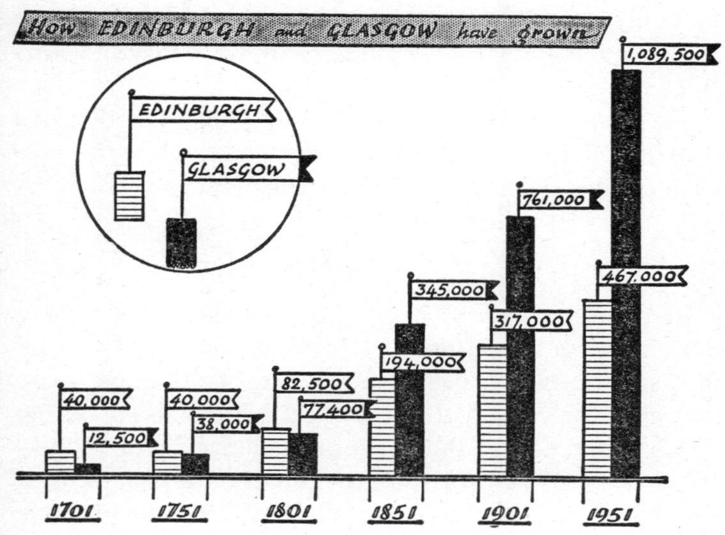

Linen-Making

For centuries women had spun woollen and linen thread to be woven into cloth for their own dresses and shawls and for the shirts and suits of their menfolk. After 1707, however, many Scots preferred the cheaper and better English woollen cloth.

But linen-making flourished, especially in Fife, Forfar and Perthshire. Flax was difficult to grow and preparing it for spinning was a messy business. So some merchants sent packmen round the countryside with linen yarn for the women to spin at home. The packmen later collected the thread and took it to towns where men weavers wove it into cloth. The government encouraged the linen industry and weavers from France and Holland were brought over to show Scots weavers how to make finer cloth. Some settled outside Edinburgh in the district still called Picardy Place.

In 1746 some big linen merchants joined together and formed the British Linen Company, and the British Linen Bank is one of the big Scottish banks today.

Trading in Tobacco

Between 1700 and 1770 Glasgow began to grow quickly. Her merchants built up huge fortunes trading in tobacco and sugar. Several Glasgow street names—Virginia Street, Jamaica Street and Tobago Street—remind us of this trade with the west. But when the American War of Independence broke out in 1776, the tobacco trade was cut off for a time, and the rich 'tobacco lords' looked for some other way to invest their money. They did not put it all in the old linen industry because cotton looked much more promising.

Cotton-Making

For a long while cotton had been spun and woven in Lancashire, for in its moist climate the threads did not break easily. At the time of the American War of Independence, Lancashire men invented new spinning machines. James Hargreaves of Blackburn made his 'spinning jenny' which spun eighty reels of thread at a time. Then Richard Arkwright, from Preston, invented a machine which spun very strong twisted thread, so that a cloth could be made of cotton alone instead of a mixture of cotton and linen. This machine was called a waterframe because it was driven by water power. After James Watt of Greenock improved the steam engine, these new machines used steam power.

During the American War of Independence, Glasgow merchants realised that in Lanarkshire and Renfrewshire the climate was suitable for spinning cotton; and the raw cotton could be brought very easily into the Clyde. The first cotton mill was built at Rothesay in 1779, but the best known one was built at New Lanark by David Dale of Glasgow, helped by his friend Arkwright. Later on, Dale was joined by Robert Owen, whose work we will talk about later.

After that the cotton industry grew and grew until by 1800 it was by far the biggest industry in Scotland. But after about fifty years came tragedy. The Civil War in

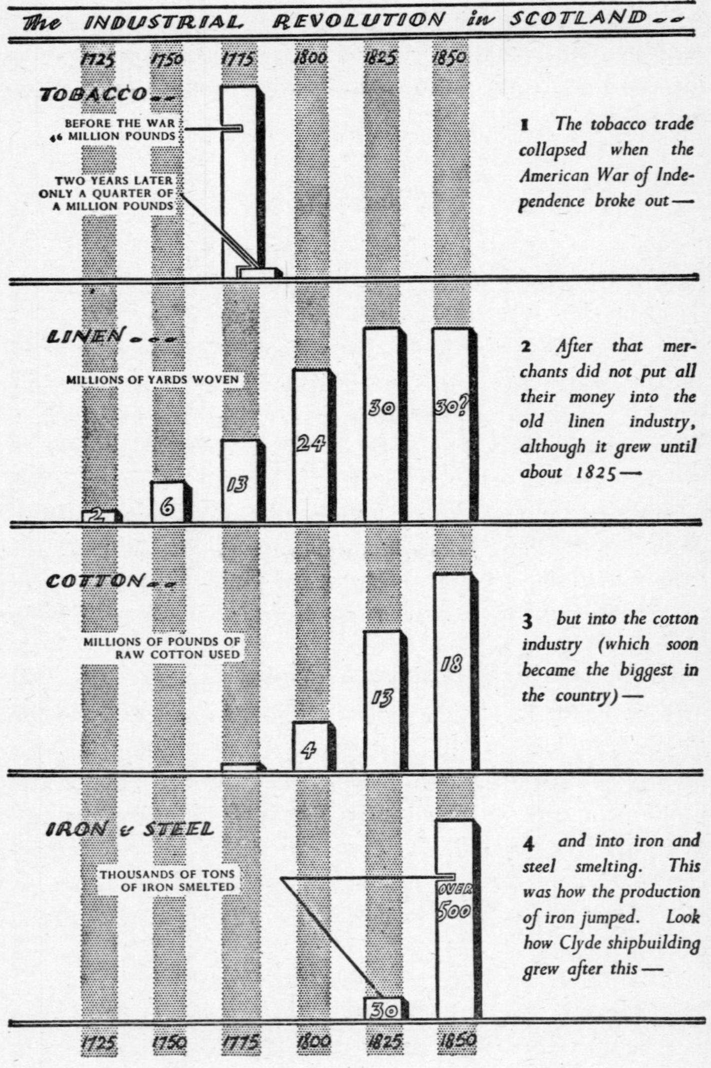

1 *The tobacco trade collapsed when the American War of Independence broke out—*

2 *After that merchants did not put all their money into the old linen industry, although it grew until about 1825—*

3 *but into the cotton industry (which soon became the biggest in the country)—*

4 *and into iron and steel smelting. This was how the production of iron jumped. Look how Clyde shipbuilding grew after this—*

America cut off the supply of cotton. After the war, the industry was built up in Lancashire, but not in the Clyde Valley. There the iron industry was growing rapidly.

Smelting and Using Iron

Iron had been mined in small quantities in the south of Scotland since very early times, but there were no real iron-works until after the Union of 1707. In England, the supply of wood for charcoal to smelt the iron was running short. So English ironmasters began to set up furnaces in the Highlands, of all places. There, there was plenty of timber and the heavy iron could be taken by boat up rivers and lochs. The first works were at Invergarry in Inverness-shire and others were soon built beside the lochs of the west Highlands.

But not long after the Union, an Englishman, Abraham Darby, showed how to smelt iron with coke, made from coal, instead of with charcoal. Now it was known that Scotland had plenty of coal and that there were deposits

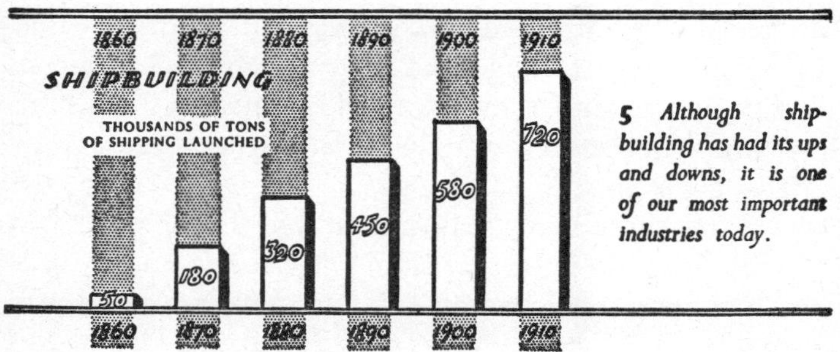

5 *Although shipbuilding has had its ups and downs, it is one of our most important industries today.*

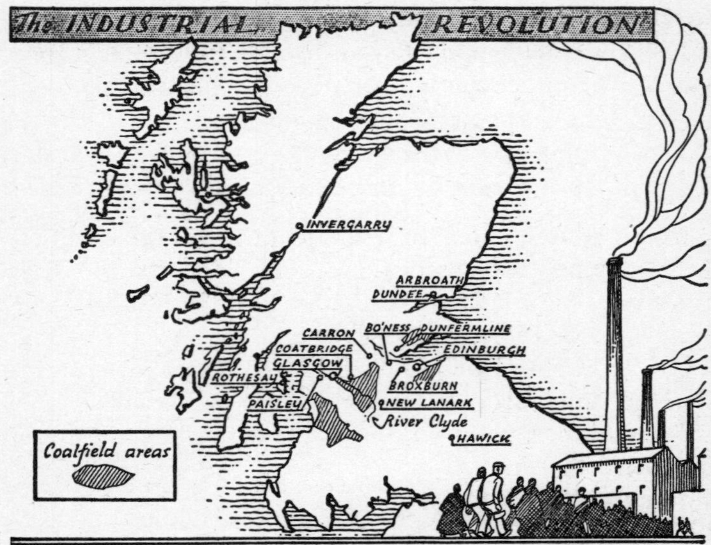

of iron ore round about Bo'ness. So in 1759 a large ironworks was set up at Carron on the Forth. Soon it became famous for the making of a naval gun called the carronade.

The works grew quickly, but there were two drawbacks. The local iron ore was not very good, and most of the ore used had to be imported. Secondly, Scots coal was not very suitable for making coke. Why, then, did the iron industry in Scotland grow so quickly between 1825 and 1850? And why did it grow up in the west when it had really started on the Forth?

There are three main reasons for this. First, very rich iron ore was found in the parish of Old Monkland. In 1825 it was a farming district with a few hundred people. Twenty years later, eight thousand people lived in the new town of Coatbridge, most of the men working in the iron furnaces. Secondly, James Neilson found that Scots coal could be used for smelting, in place of coke—if instead of cold air you blew very hot air into the furnace.

The third reason for the huge growth of the iron industry was that, as time went on, more and more iron was needed —for the new machines in cotton factories and many other things. About 1840 (as we shall see) the railway age began, and just at this time Scots iron-works began to use the inventions of Henry Cort, which allowed better iron to be made more cheaply. In 1856 Henry Bessemer showed how some of the impurities could be taken out of iron quite cheaply so that steel, which had always been very scarce and dear, now became far more plentiful and cheap. After 1860, then, iron and steel were used for a great many purposes. In Scotland the Clydeside shipbuilding industry grew rapidly, as you can see from the diagram on page 103.

Coal Mining

All this meant that more and more coal was needed to smelt the iron and feed the steam engines. Until about 1800 the only big mines were on the east coast, nearly all in Fife. When the new iron-works in Lanarkshire needed much more coal, mining began there and in Ayrshire. We shall talk more about coal mining in the next chapter.

In this chapter we have seen how some of the industries of Scotland were born and began to grow. Try to find out all you can about our industries today, and especially about those near you, or the one which gives your father work. There are some ideas to help you in the 'Things To Do.'

THINGS TO DO

1. Write one sentence about each of the following: Hargreaves, Arkwright, Dale, Derby, Neilson, Bessemer.

2. Try to find out more about the work of James Watt and the first steam engines.

3. Write paragraphs on:

(*a*) The rise and fall of the tobacco trade.
(*b*) Clydeside and cotton.
(*c*) The iron and steel industry.

4. We have read about the biggest industries, but there are many that we have not even mentioned. You could find out about some of these:

(*a*) The woollen industry of the Borders.
(*b*) Oil-shale mining in West Lothian.
(*c*) Paisley shawls and threads.
(*d*) The linen industry of Arbroath, Dundee or Dunfermline.

5. Wherever you live, find out what effect the Industrial Revolution has had in your own district.

14

Life in Factory and Mine

WE HAVE seen that more and more coal was needed after about 1760 to smelt iron and drive steam engines. Coal had been used in Scotland for many centuries before this: the monks of Newbattle Abbey were digging for it 500 years before. But the early diggings were like quarries, not pits, and the amount of coal found was very small.

So when more coal was needed, men dug tunnels into the earth from the quarries. This was dangerous work, because the earth was always falling into the tunnel. Later they dug deeper and this brought greater difficulties and greater danger. Water seeped into the bottom of the pits, poisonous and explosive gases collected, and taking the coal to the surface was hard work.

Slowly the dangers were overcome. Miners became more skilful at supporting the roofs of the tunnels, and engineers began to use steam engines to pump the water out. They lit fires at the bottom of pit shafts to drive out foul air; and Sir Humphry Davy invented a lamp which would not set fire to explosive gases. But although some improvements were made, the mines were terrible places to work in.

The hauling of coal to the surface was done by women and boys and girls—some of them quite young. Where the tunnels were high enough, women and girls carried the

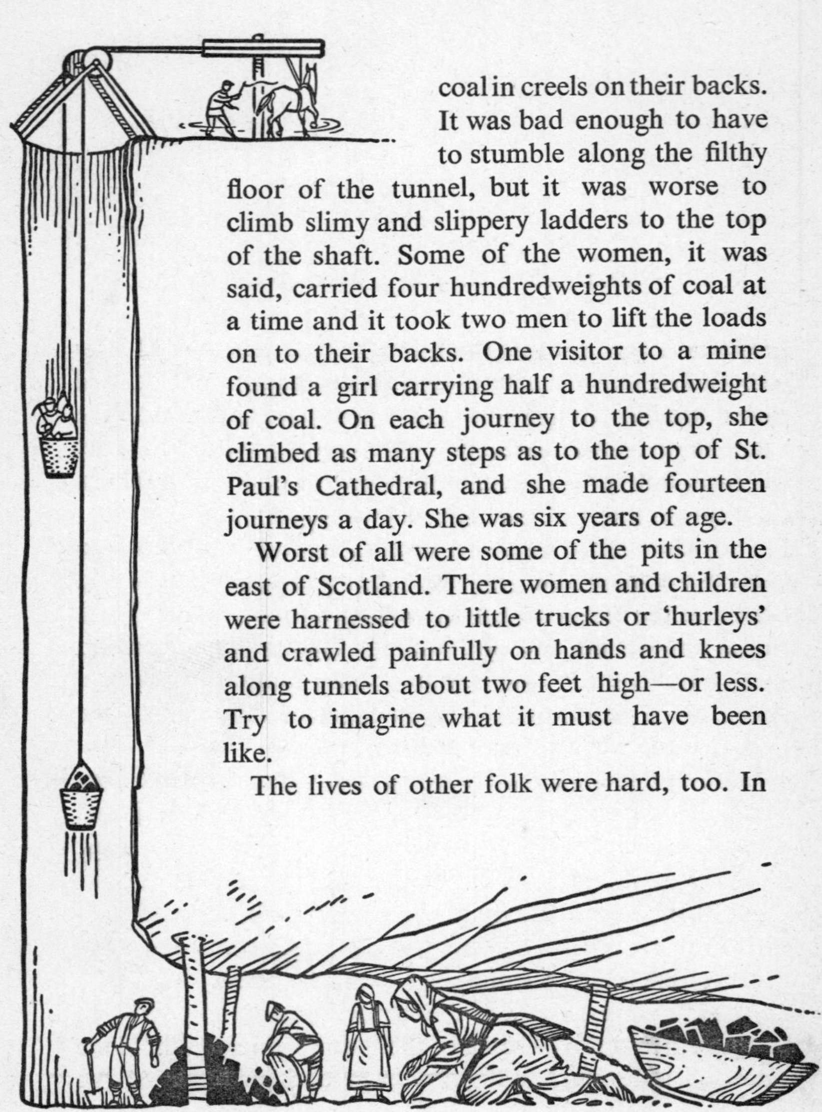

coal in creels on their backs. It was bad enough to have to stumble along the filthy floor of the tunnel, but it was worse to climb slimy and slippery ladders to the top of the shaft. Some of the women, it was said, carried four hundredweights of coal at a time and it took two men to lift the loads on to their backs. One visitor to a mine found a girl carrying half a hundredweight of coal. On each journey to the top, she climbed as many steps as to the top of St. Paul's Cathedral, and she made fourteen journeys a day. She was six years of age.

Worst of all were some of the pits in the east of Scotland. There women and children were harnessed to little trucks or 'hurleys' and crawled painfully on hands and knees along tunnels about two feet high—or less. Try to imagine what it must have been like.

The lives of other folk were hard, too. In

the big new cotton mills of Lancashire and the west of Scotland, men, women and children worked long hours in stifling factories for little pay. Many children were 'piecers': that is, they stood by a machine and when a thread snapped they tied the broken ends together. You may remember that David Livingstone, the missionary, began work at the age of ten as a piecer in a mill at Blantyre.

But perhaps the children with the very hardest lives of all were the chimney boys who swept the twisting narrow chimneys that a brush could not reach. We hear of boys who had pins stuck in the soles of their feet to make them go up chimneys a foot square. It was not uncommon for unfortunate lads to be stuck in a flue and suffocated by a fall of soot. All of them became deformed, with horrible scars or sores on knees and elbows.

HAULING COAL BEFORE 1842

About this time William Wilberforce was trying to persuade Parliament to set free the slaves in the British Empire. But many folk in Britain were probably much worse off than slaves. A master usually saw that his slaves were housed and fed properly, because they were his property.

A CLIMBING BOY AND HIS MASTER

He had paid for them, and he did not want to let them become ill and unfit to work. In Britain, few employers bothered about the life and health of their workers. They could always find another if one fell ill.

There were a few exceptional millowners, such as Robert Owen, whose New Lanark cotton mill we have already mentioned. He saw that his workers were properly housed and worked in decent conditions, and that their children were educated. Some mine owners such as the Earl of Dalkeith set an example by building pleasant cottages for their workers and looking after them and their families when they needed help.

But there were few men like Owen. Something had to be done to force all employers to shorten hours and to stop putting women and children on hard, back-breaking work. The only way this could be done was by passing Acts in Parliament. The man who did more than anyone else to persuade Parliament to pass Factory Acts and Mines Acts was Lord Shaftesbury. He was a landowner, a rich man, who need not have bothered at all about poor folk in factories and mines. But he made it his life's work to improve their lot.

At first things were very difficult for men like Wilberforce and Shaftesbury. Few people could vote in elections for Parliament: and they and their M.P.s did not care much about folk less fortunate than themselves. But a change began in 1832: Parliament passed an Act which gave more men the vote, and M.P.s began to listen more to those who wanted to improve things at home and abroad.

So in the very next year, 1833, Parliament passed a Factory Act and an Act to end slavery. The Factory Act said that children under nine were not to work at all, and that working hours for women and young folk were to be shortened. This was now the law of the land, and if a factory inspector found an employer breaking the law, the employer would be prosecuted and punished. Shaftesbury had a longer struggle before a Mines Act was passed in 1842, which stopped women and children from working underground at all. It was a longer struggle still before the evil use of climbing boys was finally ended in 1875.

During the time that Shaftesbury and others were trying to persuade Parliament to help factory and mine workers, these workers were trying to help themselves. They banded together in workers' societies—which we now call trade unions. These early trade unions tried to persuade employers to improve the conditions of work in their mines and factories. But it was an unlucky time. In the years after 1789, the British governments were terrified that a revolution like the French one would happen here. They thought these early trade unions might lead to trouble in this country, so they said workers must not join together.

When the workers could not get what they wanted peacefully, they began to listen to other leaders. The cotton spinners of Glasgow and Paisley began to use violent methods and were severely punished, sometimes by 'transportation'—by being sent to do hard labour in convict settlements overseas. Some hoped to overthrow the government by force, and they were encouraged by spies working for the government, who wanted to make an example of their leaders. In 1820 about a hundred men, with almost useless weapons, marched towards the Carron works to capture guns there. At Bonnymuir, near Falkirk, they were easily scattered by a troop of mounted soldiers, and afterwards three of their leaders were sentenced to death.

But gradually the rest of the nation saw that these workers' unions were not like the societies in France before the Revolution. So Parliament passed Acts which said that trade unions were lawful. After this their numbers grew. At first it was the more educated, skilled workmen who joined together in trade unions, but towards the end of the nineteenth century the unskilled, poorer paid men found leaders. One of these was John Burns, a leader of the dockers, and a son of Scots parents living in London. Another was Keir Hardie, from Laighbrannoch near Holytown in Lanarkshire, who began work in Glasgow when he was seven.

By this time, working-class men had been given the vote and they wanted to have their own M.P.s. So a group of Scots leaders began to plan an 'Independent Labour Party' and the idea spread to England. The first working-men members of Parliament were elected in 1892. They were John Burns and Keir Hardie. Another leader of the early Labour Party was Ramsay MacDonald, who had been a poor boy in Lossiemouth. Forty years later he became the first Labour Prime Minister.

Remember that Britain was the first country in the world to make the new iron machines and build new factories. These brought many difficulties, and the answers to these had to be found as time went on. Parliament has passed many Factory and Mines Acts to protect the health and safety of the worker. Employers today realise that people cannot work well unless they are contented. Trade unions try to make sure that their members' pay and conditions steadily improve. Some things still remain to be done and new difficulties arise now and again. But just stop to think how much better life in factory and mine is today than it was 100 or 150 years ago.

THINGS TO DO

1. Make a heading in your notebook 'How the lives of factory and mine workers have been improved' and write a paragraph about each of the following:
   (*a*) Owen and his New Lanark mill.
   (*b*) Shaftesbury and Factory and Mines Acts.
   (*c*) Trade Unions and the beginning of the Labour Party: John Burns and Keir Hardie.

2. Does your father work in a factory or mine? Try to find out from him or anyone else you know about the laws that protect folk at their work.

3. Find out all you can about trade unions today. If your father is a member of one, ask him how it works and what it is trying to do today.

4. Try to find out more about the lives of some of the workers of 150 years ago. If you live in towns such as Glasgow, Paisley or Tranent, find out all you can about work and happenings in your own district.

15

Life in the Towns

BETWEEN 1760 and 1860 a very great change took place in England. Before 1760 most Englishmen lived in the fertile lands of the south. When they began to use steam engines and iron machines the factories had to be built where coal was plentiful—in the Midlands and North England. So folk moved north to find work and out of small villages grew big towns like Leeds. Factories were built quickly; houses for the working folk were built even more quickly—and often very badly.

In Scotland things were rather different. Some towns did grow up rapidly from little villages. We have mentioned one of these, Coatbridge, which grew up where iron was found. But most of Scotland's big towns have grown out of the small trading burghs of earlier times: Edinburgh, Glasgow, Dundee, Paisley, Perth, Aberdeen. In such burghs the coming of steam power meant that the old industries were carried on in new factories, and other industries were brought in.

The best example of a small trading burgh which has grown into a big modern trading and manufacturing city is Glasgow. At the time of the Union of 1707, Glasgow was a clean and pretty little town with places and streets that remind us of a Scots burgh in Queen Mary's time. If

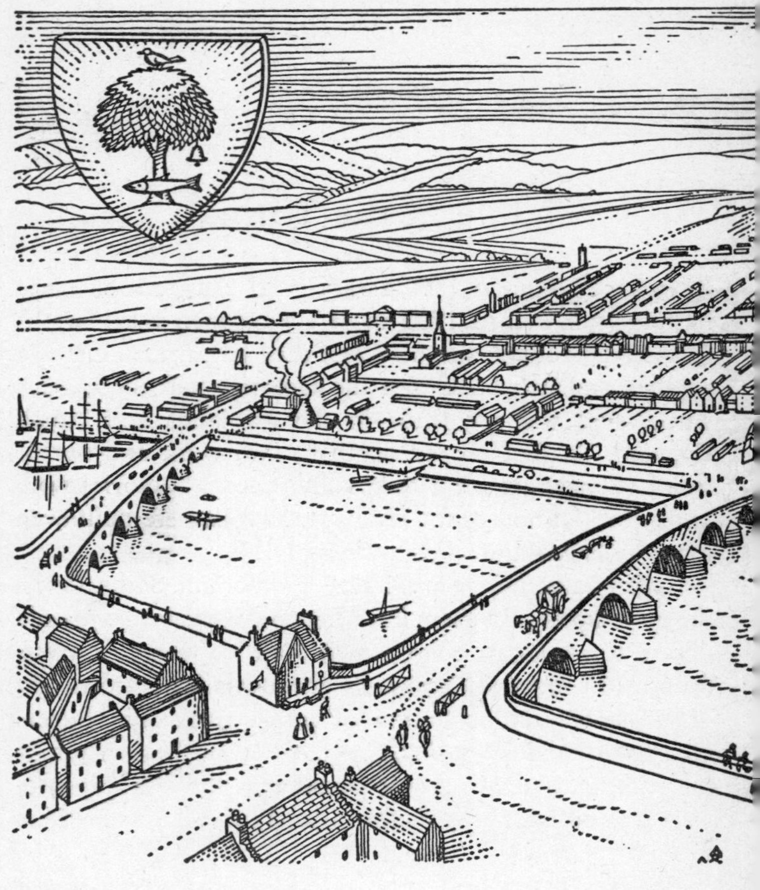

you arrived from the south of the Clyde, you would cross the bridge by the pleasant district of Gorbells and walk by the Briggate and the Saltmarket to the High Street.

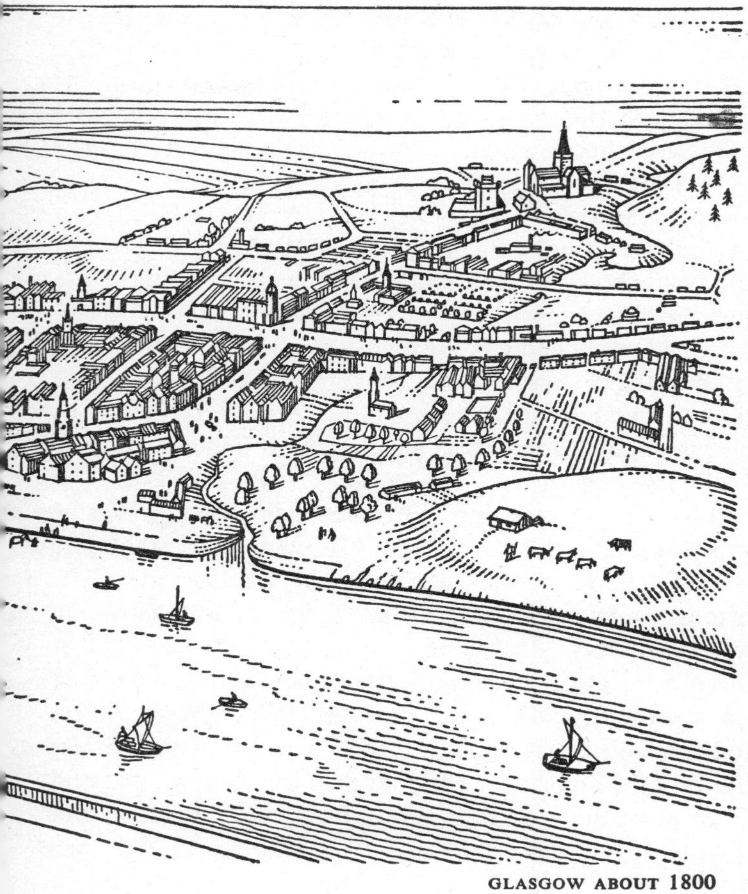

GLASGOW ABOUT 1800

You would probably pause at the Cross by the Trongate and the Gallowgate before you climbed up the High Street past the College to the Cathedral on the hill.

But already Glasgow was growing. The old Broomielaw quay was made bigger. During the eighteenth century more quays were built, the river was deepened, and trade increased. At the same time cotton mills and shipbuilding yards grew in size and number.

In 1707 about 13,000 folk lived in the little town of Glasgow. In Edinburgh there were over 40,000. Edinburgh had grown up along the 'Royal Mile', along the ridge from the Castle down to Holyrood. On each side were tall tenements or 'lands', some about ten stories high (see Plate 5). Originally they had enclosed gardens or 'closes' stretching behind them, but during the eighteenth century more houses were built in these, and now we think of a 'close' as a passageway leading to a courtyard surrounded by houses built close together.

About 1760 an English preacher named John Wesley visited Edinburgh and said that 'the chief street stank like a sewer'. This was not really surprising because no proper arrangements were made for sanitation or for the taking away of rubbish. It was risky to walk in the streets about ten o'clock at night, because that was the time when folk opened their windows and shot the day's rubbish out on to the cobbled street below or on to the head of any passer-by. From the duchess's maid on the top flat to the rag and bone merchant's wife at the bottom, they all cried out 'Gardyloo!' (from the French '*Gardez l'eau*', 'Mind the water') and then let it go. If a passer-by could not shout out quickly 'Haud yer han'!' or duck into the nearest doorway, it was just too bad.

As you can imagine, this made the overcrowded city a very unhealthy place to live in: especially as all the drinking

EDINBURGH'S HIGH STREET ABOUT 1800

water was drawn from public wells in the middle of the street.

In the century following the Union, Glasgow, Edinburgh and other towns became more and more crowded. Still little or nothing was done to make them healthier. Epidemics of killing diseases such as smallpox and typhus came year after year. After the awful epidemic of 1848, Parliament and the Town Councils of the big towns began to do something about it. The first Public Health Act was passed and the big cities were compelled to arrange proper sanitation and safe water supplies. They began to appoint doctors as Medical Officers of Health to look after such important matters. After about 1860 some towns turned their attention to housing and began to clear away some of the worst slums.

In the biggest towns there were ‘poorhouses’ for folk who were poor and unemployed, and there were ‘hospitals’ for the old people and for orphans. But in most towns and all the country parishes, people had to pay a ‘poor rate’ or ‘poor tax’. Unemployed and old folk were given money and continued to stay in their own homes. In addition, towns and parishes gave licences to some poor men and women to beg. The ‘gaberlunzie man’ with his blue gown and big licence-badge was quite a common sight.

The licensed beggars were not lawless folk, but it is not surprising that in the towns growing up between 1760 and 1860 there were people guilty of crimes. In the towns the bailies, and in the counties the sheriffs, saw that law and order were kept. There were few police forces in Scotland before about 1850: in Edinburgh, for example, there was just the ‘City Guard’ made up of tired old soldiers.

Prisoners were taken to the Tolbooth prison or to the Sheriff Court House for trial. Punishments were severe: a man could be sentenced to several years in a convict settlement overseas—for sheep stealing.

Later a man could be sure of fairer treatment. In 1822 Sir Robert Peel had begun the Metropolitan Police in London and after about 1850 burghs and counties in Scotland set up their own police forces. After 1850, too, a wrongdoer was always brought first before Bailies in the Burgh Court or the Sheriff in his court. If the Sheriff thought a heavier punishment than he could give was needed, he would send the case to be tried by a jury in a court presided over by a High Court judge. This is what happens today.

How did folk spend their spare time? They had never had very much: work was hard and long, and was even longer after the coming of factories. The old feast days were the main rests from work: Fastern's E'en or Shrove Tuesday, Beltane, May Day, Hallow'en, Hogmanay and New Year's Day. Some of the towns had Fair Weeks. The fairs had begun as trading markets but became just amusement fairs, with all kinds of stalls, amusing oddities, and much noise. The Glasgow holiday week, for example, is still called 'The Fair' although no fair is held today. Other towns had celebrations of their own, such as the Riding of the Marches at Linlithgow and Hawick. In some places, horse-racing, golf, shinty, were popular; in others, handball and football. Perhaps you have heard of the game still played every year at Jedburgh between the 'Uppies' and the 'Doonies'.

And in these towns where there was much hard work and

misery and some fun, there were men whose names and work live on today. Some of Scotland's greatest writers lived in Edinburgh between 1770 and 1800. Robert Burns, from Alloway in Ayrshire, stayed in the city in 1786. A few years earlier died Robert Fergusson, the poet who left stirring examples of poetry in the Scots tongue which inspired Burns. Shortly after Burns visited Edinburgh, young Walter Scott attended the Royal High School there. About the same time lived the architect Robert Adam and the great portrait-painter, Sir Henry Raeburn. It was Adam who designed Charlotte Square in Edinburgh (Plate 6), said to be one of the finest in Europe.

In Glasgow, about the same time, the first technical college in Europe was begun by Professor John Anderson, who had helped James Watt in his work on the steam engine. Another of the many Glasgow scientists of the time was Joseph Black, whom you may have heard about in your science lessons. Another teacher was Adam Smith, a professor at the University, who wrote an important book called *The Wealth of Nations* which gave many men new ideas about the importance of trade between countries.

* * *

Life in the towns between 1707 and 1850 meant different things for different people. For some there were meetings with great men: writers, artists, scientists. For others there was comfort and luxury, since trade and profits were bigger than ever. For many there was just misery and hard work, dirt and disease, sickness and sadness.

But slowly, as we have seen, things began to improve.

Towns became cleaner and healthier, lawbreakers were dealt with more fairly, and the towns we know took shape. In them much has been done to improve people's lives—but much still remains to be done.

THINGS TO DO

1. Why was there so much disease and ill-health in Scots towns in the eighteenth and nineteenth centuries? Write down as many reasons as you can.

2. If you live near Glasgow, or Edinburgh, look carefully at the drawing showing your city about 1800 and write a paragraph about it.

3. Explain: 'Gardyloo!', sanitation, 'gaberlunzie man', City Guard, Fastern's E'en, Beltane, Glasgow Fair, 'land', 'close'.

4. Find out all you can about the lives and writings of Fergusson, Burns and Scott. You should know some of the poems of Fergusson and Burns and some of Scott's novels. Write down the names of some of them in your notebook.

5. Try to find out more about the work of Robert Adam, Sir Henry Raeburn, Joseph Black and Adam Smith.

6. Do you know what happens in a court of law? What kind of cases are tried in the Court of Session and in the Court of Justiciary?

16

The Work of the Churches

THE first thing to notice is the title of this chapter. In Book One we read about the work of 'the Church', the Catholic world-wide church. In the eighteenth century, long after the Reformation, we talk of churches: Roman Catholic, Episcopalian, Presbyterian and others. In Scotland there were many faithful members of the Roman Catholic and Episcopal Churches, but most folk belonged to the Presbyterian 'Church of Scotland' founded on the teaching of Calvin and Knox.

Before the Reformation the Catholic Church had played a most important part in the life and work of the nation. At abbeys such as Melrose the sick were cared for; the poor and unemployed were given help; and travellers were sheltered. Churchmen taught the young and wrote books. Bishops helped kings to govern their kingdoms and even ruled when kings were too young to do so. But, as we have seen, the Church became too rich and attracted the wrong kind of men.

After the Reformation a great deal of the riches of the Catholic Church passed into the hands of lairds and nobles. So the new Presbyterian Church was not able to do all it planned to do, even as late as the eighteenth century. However, it did continue some of the work of the old Catholic Church. Each parish helped its own poor, and each church had its 'poor box' in which money was collected for them. Kirk sessions raised money for the poor in other ways, as we shall see. Again, John Knox had hoped that each parish would have a school of its own. It was more than 200 years before this came about, but by 1750 practically every parish had its own school and dominie. The dominie was always a leading member of the parish church and the minister took a great interest in the school. A very important occasion was his visit to hear the pupils give the answers to the Catechism.

Altogether the Church in the eighteenth century had a great hold over ordinary folk. Unfortunately many ministers and elders were narrow-minded men with very strict views about what was proper behaviour. On the Sabbath, they said, no work whatever was to be done, and there were two two-hour services in the cold and comfortless kirk: one in the morning and one in the afternoon. In several towns elders known as 'seizers' searched the streets, and even the houses, for folk who were absent from kirk. These and other cases of misbehaviour (such as drunkenness and swearing) were reported to the kirk session and were punished by them. Offenders might be fined—the money went to help the poor—and often they were sentenced to 'stand at the pillory'. This meant that the man (or woman) stood, clad only in a rough gown of sackcloth, at the church door while folk filed in for the service. Worse still, during the service he had to remain on the 'cutty stool' in front of the congregation, while the minister thundered at him from the pulpit.

These long services in church were important affairs:

but even more important were the communion services held once or twice a year. To these 'Occasions', as they

ON THE CUTTY STOOL

were called, came people from neighbouring parishes—and from further afield. Later in the eighteenth century they became more like public holidays. Robert Burns described the folk at one in his poem *Holy Fair*:

Here some are thinking on their sins
An' some upon their claes;
Ane curses feet that fyl'd his shins,
Another sighs and prays;
On this hand sits a chosen swatch
Wi' screwed-up, grace-prood faces;
On that a set o' chaps, at watch,
Thrang winkin' on the lasses.

It is easy to criticise ministers and elders of the eighteenth century because they were different from those we know today. But we must remember that there were reasons for what they did. In the eighteenth century ministers preached long sermons on the Bible because they believed the Word of God was all-important. They made their people obey a very strict discipline because they felt that the behaviour of most people needed improvement. They made Communion services great occasions because they wanted folk to feel how important these services were.

Often when people want to change something they change too much. By about 1800 many younger ministers felt that these ways were too strict. They saw nothing wrong in novels, plays and theatre-going. One of them, the Rev. John Home of Athelstaneford in East Lothian, even wrote a play, a tragedy called *Douglas*. Card-playing, to these ministers, was a pleasant pastime, not a dangerous meddling with the 'de'il's books'. These men were called 'Moderates' and they led the way towards the less strict kind of Sunday most of us spend today.

A great split known as the 'Disruption' took place in the Church of Scotland in the nineteenth century. A large group of ministers and their congregations left it and set up their own churches. Why did they do this? After 1690 it was the custom in the Presbyterian Church for the congregations to choose their minister. After the Union, however, Parliament passed the Patronage Act, which gave back to the local landowner, or 'patron', power to appoint the minister he wanted. This led to a great deal of trouble, and long afterwards, in 1843, Dr. Thomas Chalmers led more than a third of the ministers out of the Church of

Scotland to set up a new Free Church. They believed in choosing their own ministers and did not think that Parliament had any right to tell them what to do.

At last, Acts were passed to end the landowners' power to appoint parish ministers and to end Parliament's right to decide church matters. So in 1929 most of the 'Free' churches were joined again to the Church of Scotland.

Today the government and Parliament have nothing to do with the Church of Scotland. The Queen is not head of the Church as she is head of the Church of England, but every year she sends her representative to the General Assembly. He is called the 'Lord High Commissioner' and during Assembly time he lives at Holyrood Palace, but he does not take part in the debates. The president of the Assembly is called the Moderator of the General Assembly and is chosen each year from among leading ministers of the Church. (See Plate 7.)

* * *

We have not said much about two other Churches in Scotland: the Roman Catholic Church and the Episcopal Church. Today, of course, everyone is allowed to worship as he likes and to belong to the Church of his choice. But it was not always so, even in quite recent times. You will remember that Roman Catholics and Episcopalians were harshly treated after the Scots Kirk became presbyterian. Later, many of them were supporters of the Jacobite cause, and things were made even more difficult for them because their loyalty was suspected. It was not until 1858, for example, that Episcopalians were allowed to attend Scottish universities.

Today the Episcopal Church is strong in the north-east, especially in Aberdeenshire and in the Highlands, but its churches are found all over the country. They are ruled by their bishops, seven in number, and they use in their services a prayer-book rather like the one used in the Church of England.

Catholics used to be most numerous in the Highlands, where the Jacobites found most of their support. Feeling against them was sometimes very strong, not only in Scotland but in England too. About 1780 there were big anti-Popish riots in London, and in Edinburgh a Catholic chapel was burnt down. Many Catholics emigrated, especially to North America.

Many more came over to Scotland from Ireland to find work in the growing towns of the west, and this is where most Scots Catholics live today. The Roman Catholic Church in Scotland is organised under two archbishops, one of St. Andrews and Edinburgh and the other of Glasgow, and six other bishops. In many towns, as you probably know, there are separate Roman Catholic schools.

All these Churches and other organisations—especially the Salvation Army—did much good work in the growing towns of the nineteenth century. Today we see new districts and even new towns growing up. In these the Churches are carrying on 'extension' work and building new churches where they are needed most.

THINGS TO DO

1. Explain the meanings of: poor box, dominie, Shorter Catechism, seizers, cutty stool, Occasions, disrupt.

2. Write a sentence about each of the following: Patronage Act, Disruption, Moderator of the General Assembly, Lord High Commissioner.

3. Find out all you can about the history of your own church or the one nearest your school.

4. When the General Assembly of the Church of Scotland meets, make a collection of newspaper cuttings showing its work.

17

Roads, Railways and Steamships

YOU will have read a lot about space travel. As you read this, scientists are working in their laboratories trying to bring nearer the time when men will journey to the moon. Yet have you ever thought that it is not much more than fifty years since the first aeroplanes, and little more than a hundred years since the first railways? As you can see, there have been wonderful changes in ways of travel in recent times.

Two hundred years ago, there were not even any properly made, hard surface roads in Britain. The last good roads had been built by the Romans thirteen hundred years before! Travellers and goods were carried on horseback: and long, uncomfortable journeys they were. It took days for goods from Edinburgh to reach Selkirk. It took a day and a half to travel between Glasgow and Edinburgh; and about a fortnight to reach London.

The first improvements were made by two Scotsmen: Thomas Telford from Westerkirk in Dumfriesshire, and John Macadam of Ayr. Telford built roads, canals and bridges all over the country. For example, he built the Menai Suspension Bridge, the Caledonian Canal and St. Katherine Docks, London. Macadam was a great road-builder whose methods are still used in making our 'macadamised' roads. Nowadays we bind the smaller stones of the surface together with tar and call it 'tar-macadam'.

Over these roads travel was faster. By about 1780 you could travel between Glasgow and Edinburgh in twelve hours, and to London in two and a half days.

About the same time as these roads were being built, factory and mine owners found a new, cheap way of carry-

A STAGECOACH

ing their heavy goods. They began to make and use canals, artificial waterways. The first in Britain was made by an Englishman, James Brindley, at Manchester. Later in Scotland the Forth and Clyde, Union, and Crinan canals were built. (Make sure that you know where these are and why they were built.) As well as building canals, the channels of rivers—especially the Clyde—were deepened so that they could be used by sea-going ships.

For many years some of the Scottish collieries had used 'waggonways', rails along which horses pulled the coal wagons. One of these, at Tranent, was opened in 1745, and soon after this they became quite common in the Ayrshire and Lanarkshire coalfields. So it is not surprising that the first locomotives, or steam-engines on wheels, were used at these collieries where there were already rails and plenty of coal. The first locomotive was made by Richard Trevithick in 1804, but the best known engine-builder was George Stephenson. The first railway in Scotland was opened in 1824; and it carried coal from the Monkland collieries to the Forth and Clyde Canal at Kirkintilloch.

At first nobody thought of using railways to carry passengers, but in 1831 the first passenger line in Scotland was opened. George Stephenson himself drove the first train along it from Glasgow to Garnkirk in Lanarkshire. But many people distrusted new inventions, and the new railways and engines had many enemies. Among these were the owners of the Forth and Clyde Canal and the Town Council of Linlithgow. The canal owners tried to prevent the building of a railway from Glasgow to Edinburgh—because it would take business away from the canal. At Linlithgow, the Town Council tried to make the railway pay for all the goods it carried through the town: just like the 'dues' that 'foreign' merchants had to pay in earlier times.

But people slowly realised the advantage of railways, and thousands of miles of track were laid about the middle of the century. Railway-building was a costly business, of course. The first big stations were built at Haymarket, Edinburgh, and Queen Street, Glasgow; and bridges were built across the rivers Tay and Forth. At the same time, improvements were made for the safety and comfort of passengers.

At one time there were about fifty railway companies in

THE OPENING OF THE RAILWAY FROM GARNKIRK TO COATBRIDGE 1831

Scotland, many of them very small, but by 1900 there were only five big ones. The map on page 136 will show you where their trains ran. Later these companies were swallowed up by the London, Midland and Scottish (L.M.S.) and the London and North Eastern Railway (L.N.E.R.). Now, as you know, all railways are 'nationalised'; they belong to the State, and are known as British Railways.

The steam-engine not only brought great changes in land travel but it completely altered sea travel too. Until the nineteenth century, ships had been made of wood and had used sails, but about 1850 big sailing ships called 'clippers' were built of iron. These ships were very fast and were used to race the new season's tea crop back from China. Many of them were built at Aberdeen and some at Greenock. One very famous clipper, the *Cutty Sark*, was made at Dumbarton. They must have been a wonderful sight as they sped along, crowded with sails, but they were the last of the great sailing ships.

For long before the age of clippers, men were experimenting with steam-engines in ships. Some of these early experiments were made by Scotsmen, and in 1802 Andrew Symington built his tug, the *Charlotte Dundas*, at Grangemouth and showed what it could do on the Forth and Clyde Canal. Again, men were afraid of new things: the owners of the canal would not allow it to be used regularly and Symington died penniless. Meanwhile, in America, paddle steamers were being built for use on the lakes and rivers and Henry Bell of Helensburgh used these as models. His ship, the *Comet*, was launched on the Clyde in 1812 and carried passengers on the Clyde and along the west coast.

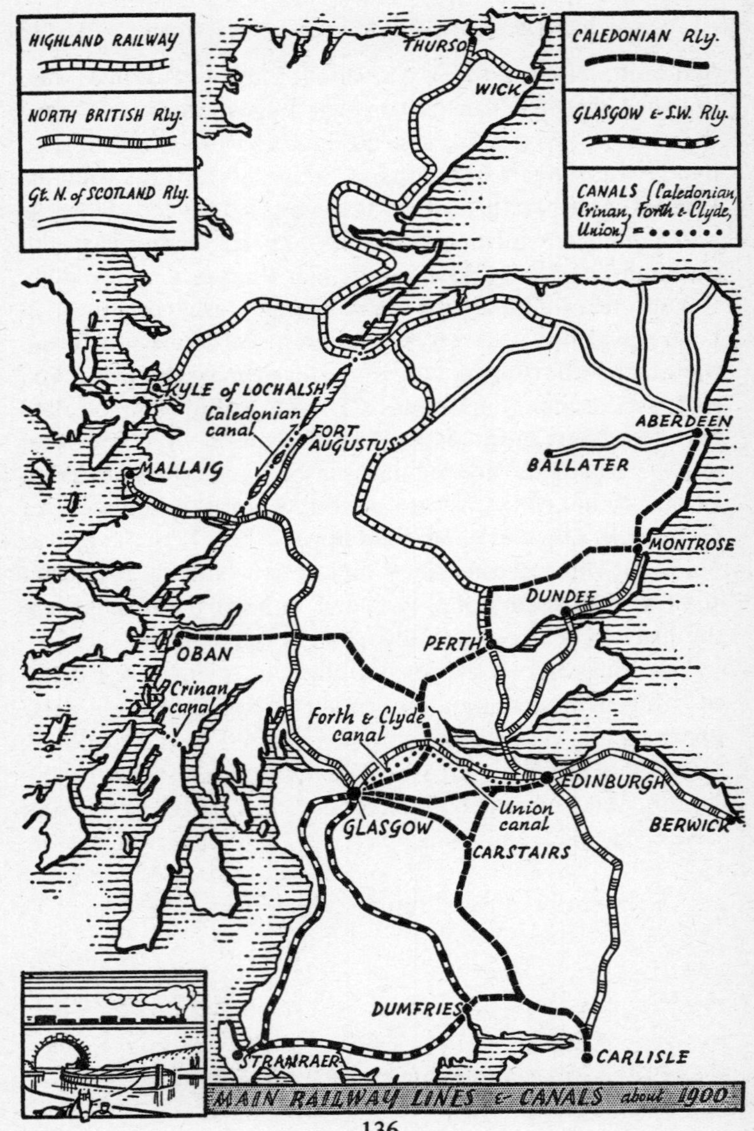

MAIN RAILWAY LINES & CANALS about 1900

One big drawback of these early steamships was that the coal fuel took up a great deal of space that could have been used for cargo. The earliest sea-going steamships like the American *Savannah*, which was the first to cross the Atlantic, carried sails in case they were needed. These coal-burning engines were gradually improved, but the problem of stowage space for fuel was not completely solved until oil-burning engines were introduced.

So the steam-engine brought the great changes of railway and steamship travel. Experiments were also made with steam-cars. They had little luck, for they were very heavy and did much damage to the roads. But they were finally 'killed' by an Act passed by Parliament in 1865. This said that they must not travel at more than two miles an hour in towns and five miles an hour in the country. As if that was not enough, each car had to have three men in charge of it, one of whom had to walk in front with a red flag!

Thus the steam-car disappeared—but before many years had passed, other cars took their place and had more success.

THINGS TO DO

1. Write a sentence about each of the following to show what important work they did: Thomas Telford, John Macadam, James Brindley, Richard Trevithick, George Stephenson, Andrew Symington, Henry Bell.

2. Write a short paragraph about:

   (*a*) Scots canals;

   (*b*) Scots railway companies before 1921;

(*c*) 'Clippers';
(*d*) The Red Flag Act.

3. On a blank map of Scotland mark in:
(*a*) Scots railways before 1921;
(*b*) The Caledonian, Crinan, and Forth and Clyde canals;
(*c*) Shipbuilding towns.

4. Find out all you can about the oldest railways in your district or town and write a short history about them.

5. If you live in Aberdeen or one of the shipbuilding towns of the west, write a short history of the shipbuilding yards there.

6. See if you can collect any pictures, photographs or relics of any of the early railways.

18

The Age of Power and Speed

ALTHOUGH steamships and steam railways were a great success, steam-cars were a failure—in Europe, anyway. But about twenty years later, in 1884, a German experimented with a petrol-engine on wheels. In other words, he began to make motor-cars, and you know his name already—Daimler. Eleven years passed before the first motor-car reached Britain, because the Red Flag Act was still in force.

However, in 1896 the law was changed and the speed limit was raised to 12 miles an hour. To celebrate this, there was a special run from London to Brighton, and this is still remembered in the 'Old Crocks' Run' every year. Although most of these early motor-cars were manufactured in France and Germany, the air-filled or pneumatic tyre was the idea of a Scot, John Dunlop, in 1888.

The Dunlop tyre was not actually produced for motor-cars but for the bone-shaking bicycles. In 1818 the 'hobby horse' was brought to Britain from France, but the first real 'bicycle' was invented twenty years later by a Scots blacksmith, Kirkpatrick Macmillan of Courthill in Dumfriesshire. Afterwards, in order to get more speed and make steering easier, the front wheel was made larger and the pedals fixed to the hub. So the 'penny farthing' was born, but later its place was taken by the 'safety bicycle' designed like the one you use.

Today both bicycles and motor-cars are mass-produced: that is, produced in great numbers cheaply and quickly. Men such as Henry Ford in America and William Morris (Lord Nuffield) in this country showed how cars could be made this way. Motoring became popular: in 1894 there was not a single motor-car in Britain, while today there are nearly four million. Motor vehicles are not just used for pleasure but are very important for the transport of workers and goods.

But we are having to pay for the progress. Every year the number of people killed and injured in road accidents goes up. This year about 5,000 people will be killed and 262,000 others injured on Britain's roads. (In an average year of the last war 50,000 British troops were killed and 50,000 were wounded.) Now you see why so much attention is being given nowadays to road safety, and how necessary it all is.

The petrol-engine brought in the age of the motor-car

—and of the aeroplane. For centuries men had dreamed of travel in the air. Before the time of Christ, the ancient Greeks told the story of Icarus, who tried to fly with wings made of feathers fixed to him with wax. You will remember that Damian in the time of James IV met with disaster. So did Icarus: he flew too near the sun and the wax melted. About 1500 Leonardo da Vinci even drew a plan for a flying-machine, but he had no powered engine to enable him to try out his idea.

About 1800 men such as the French brothers Montgolfier made ascents by balloon. When the petrol-engine was invented, the obvious thing to do was to fix one to a balloon, and from about 1900 onwards many powered balloons or 'airships' were built. One of the most famous pioneers was the German Count Zeppelin. Airships were used by both sides in the First World War and in 1919 a British airship crossed the Atlantic. But then there were a number of disasters to these gas-filled airships. After the British 'R.101' crashed on a flight over France in 1930, the days of the airship were ended.

BICYCLES OLD AND NEW

Long before this, of course, men had succeeded in flying in machines that, unlike the airships, were actually heavier than air. They were able to do so because they used a petrol-engine to drive a propeller which directed a stream of air against the wings of the aeroplane. The propeller pulled the machine forward and the stream of air pushed it upwards.

In 1903 two Americans, the brothers Wilbur and Orville Wright, made the first flight in a machine that was heavier than air. Their engine was eight horse-power—the same as a modern small car—and their longest flight was just half a mile and took less than a minute. In 1908 A. V. Roe made the first flight in England. He travelled less than a hundred yards and never rose higher than three feet.

But these were the beginning of great things. In the next year, 1909, the Frenchman Blériot crossed the English Channel. In the war of 1914–1918 both sides saw the value of aircraft for reconnaissance, artillery spotting, bombing, and fighting. The 'Royal Flying Corps' was started in 1912 and later developed into the Royal Air Force. By the end of the First World War so much progress had been made that two Englishmen, Alcock and Brown, were able to cross the Atlantic and the first passenger service (from London to Paris) began.

Between the wars there were many pioneer flights: both by R.A.F. officers and private fliers such as Sir Alan Cobham and Amy Johnson. As bigger and more reliable aircraft were built, passenger airlines spread over the routes on which the pioneers had flown.

During the war of 1939–1945 the Governments on both sides placed big orders for aircraft and encouraged scientists to experiment. Men with startling new ideas now had their chance: men such as Group Captain Frank Whittle, who invented a jet engine. As you will read later, the aeroplane played a very great part in the Second World War.

Today we have aircraft of strange new designs flying at supersonic speeds. An aircraft reached the speed of over a thousand miles an hour less than fifty years after Blériot flew at 43 m.p.h. What does the future hold? Will there really be space travel?

Scientists are sure there will. Already we are finding out what it is like in outer space. In 1957 Russia startled the world by announcing that she had sent up a 'satellite' (which they called 'Sputnik One') about five hundred miles above the earth. This was a metal case, using marvellous new fuels, which went round the earth fifteen times a day at a speed of 18,000 miles an hour.

But there are all kinds of difficulties in the way of space travel. We do not know how the 'cosmic' rays found at these great heights will affect men. In order to find out, the Russians sent up 'Sputnik Two'. This one was much bigger and carried a dog as passenger.

Once scientists have found out how men can stay alive in these conditions, human passengers will go up in satellites. Later, attempts will be made to reach the moon —and the Russians believe they will be able to do this in a few years' time.

As far as we can see, there will have to be a stop somewhere. Even at the high speeds the space ships will reach, a journey to Mars would take two years, to Venus three years. To reach a star would take a lifetime. Even though that may be impossible, the future is exciting. Try to find out all you can about travel: past, present—and future!

THINGS TO DO

1. Write a sentence about each of the following:

Kirkpatrick Macmillan, Gottlieb Daimler, J. B. Dunlop, William Morris.

The Montgolfier brothers, Count Zeppelin, Wilbur and Orville Wright, A. V. Roe, Blériot, Alcock and Brown, Frank Whittle.

2. Read more about the history of the R.A.F. and the work it has done in peace and war.

3. Find out more about the development of the aeroplane and the motor-car. (See Plates 11 and 12.)

4. Make your own, or class, books showing 'The Story of the Bicycle', 'The Story of the Motor-Car', and 'The Story of the Aeroplane'. Collect pictures of machines, from the earliest to the most modern, and write a short description of each one. When the pictures show quite a continuous story, paste them in exercise books.

5. Try to find out more about recent experiments to do with space travel.

19

The Work of Explorers

YOU will remember that the great 'discoverers' who lived about 1500 added a great deal to man's knowledge of the world. They discovered the American continent and found a way to India round the south coast of Africa. By 1800 Captain Cook had explored the coast of Australia and surveyed part of the coast of Antarctica. The outline of the map of the world was almost as we know it today.

But in 1800 a great deal of that map of the world was blank. What lay in Central Africa and Central Australia was a mystery and no man had ventured far into the ice-bound Polar regions. It was the work of men of the nineteenth and twentieth centuries to explore and map these unknown lands.

Africa

The exploration of much of Central Africa was the work of David Livingstone of Blantyre. His parents were poor and when he was ten he went to work in a cotton mill. He worked from six in the morning until eight at night, but still he managed to teach himself Latin and Greek, and to read many books on travel and science. When he was 23 he went to Glasgow University, working in the mill during his holidays to pay his fees. By the time he was 28 he had qualified as a doctor and went out to Africa as a missionary.

From Cape Town he travelled north to join the mission of a fellow-Scot, Dr. Robert Moffat, whose daughter he

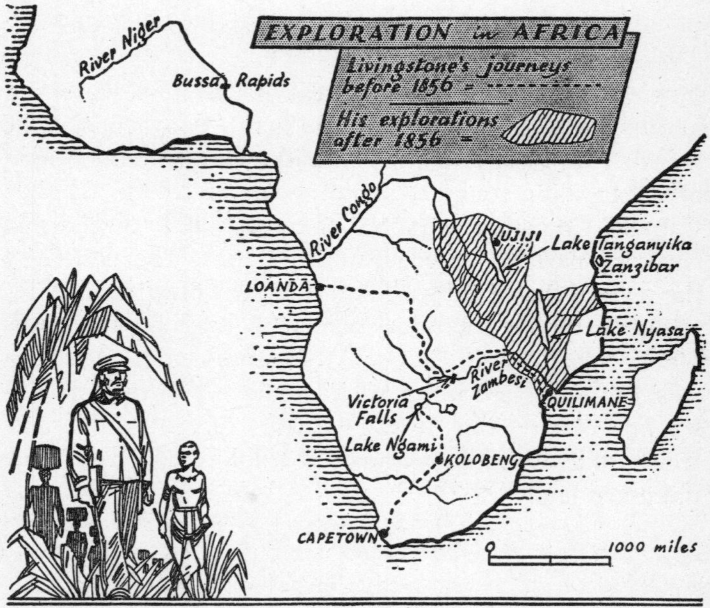

later married. But Livingstone was impatient to push on into unknown lands and meet natives who had not known the white man. He made his way north into swampy country where he discovered Lake Ngami. Further on, he reached a great river, the Zambesi.

His aim now was to pioneer new routes to the east and

the west which would be easier for missionaries and traders than the route he had followed from Kolobeng. So at Linyanti he made ready. He travelled as far as he could by canoe up the Zambesi and then he headed west through the dense forest, sometimes on foot, sometimes on oxen. Even his faithful servants had had enough and threatened to go home. But at last they reached the west coast at Loanda, a Portuguese settlement. Livingstone, weak with fever, rested a while and then returned to Linyanti.

In a few months he was off again—this time to journey east, down the Zambesi. On the way to the coast he came to a huge waterfall, where the river, over half a mile wide, suddenly drops over four hundred feet. This he named the 'Victoria Falls'. When Livingstone reached the mouth of the Zambesi, he had crossed the continent of Africa from coast to coast.

Later he explored the region from the mouth of the Zambesi to Lake Tanganyika. Often he found that the natives were unfriendly, for they thought he was one of the slave traders who attacked villages and carried off men, women and children for sale as slaves. Many of these unfortunate folk died on the way, and Livingstone said he saw 'skulls and bones scattered about everywhere'.

By this time Livingstone was famous. The outside world had heard no news of him for four years, and a New York newspaper sent out a search party under the command of Henry M. Stanley. You have probably heard the story of his meeting with Livingstone at Ujiji on the shores of Lake Tanganyika.

Livingstone refused to return home with Stanley, saying

that he had too much work to do in Africa. One morning in 1873 his native porters opened the door of his tent. They found him kneeling by the side of his bed, his head resting on his arms. The travels of David Livingstone from Blantyre were over.

But his work was carried on by Henry Stanley. Stanley had stayed with Livingstone for four months and together they had explored the country round Lake Tanganyika. Later Stanley explored the whole length of the other great river of Central Africa, the Congo. It took him nearly a year and was full of difficulties—disease, dark forest, hunger and hostile tribes.

* * *

So we have seen that Scots played a great part in missionary work and exploration in South and Central Africa. In West Africa the exploration of the River Niger was largely the work of another Scot, Mungo Park, who came from Foulshiels in Selkirkshire and was a friend of Sir Walter Scott.

In 1795 he set out on his first journey, accompanied only by a man and a boy, into unknown dangers. He was captured and imprisoned by a chief for four months. He escaped, alone, but had gone no more than a mile from his village-prison when he was overtaken by robbers who took away his only cloak. Although now he had nothing to protect him from the rains by day or from the mosquitoes by night, he pushed on and reached the River Niger. He travelled for eighty miles down the river until sheer exhaustion made him turn back. Then he fell ill of fever and stayed in the hut of a friendly negro for over six months until he recovered and was able to return to the coast and then home.

But he did not stay long in Scotland. In 1805 he went out again to West Africa. He led quite a large party this

'MR. PARK ATTEMPTED TO PASS'

time, but they met with such hardships that out of thirty-four soldiers and four carpenters who began the journey only six soldiers and one carpenter reached the Niger. But Park never dreamed of giving up, and with the help of the only other fit man he made one good boat out of two old canoes. Now he was ready for the voyage up river and with his few remaining companions he set off. Nothing more was heard from the great-hearted Mungo Park.

The end of the story was given by a man who had been Park's guide for part of the journey, and he got it from a slave who was the only survivor. The party reached the Bussa rapids, a hundred miles up the Niger. At that point, said the guide, 'there is a rock across the whole breadth of the river. One part of the rock is very high; there is a large opening in that rock in the form of a door, which is the only passage for the water to pass through; the current is here very strong. Warriors went and took possession of the top of this opening. Mr. Park came there after they had posted themselves; he nevertheless attempted to pass. The people began to attack him, throwing lances, pikes, arrows and stones. Mr. Park defended himself for a long time; two of the slaves at the stern of the canoe were killed; they threw every thing they had into the river, and kept firing; but being overpowered by numbers and fatigue, and unable to keep up the canoe against the current, and with no probability of escaping, Mr. Park took hold of one of the white men, and jumped into the water. They were drowned in the stream in attempting to escape.'

Australia

You will remember that the first British settlement in Australia was at Botany Bay, near the modern Sydney. More and more settlers came; the towns of Brisbane, Melbourne and Adelaide were founded; all on the coast.

From the east coast the way inland was blocked by an almost impassable range of mountains.

However, in 1813 there was a terrible drought and some settlers made the difficult journey over the Blue Mountains to find fresh pastures for their flocks. There they found something they had not expected. The rivers they reached did not flow east but west, and they supposed that there must be a great inland sea into which these rivers flowed. Nothing more was done to explore inland until another drought occurred in 1828.

Then the job was given to Captain Charles Sturt, who took a small party and a boat to sail on the inland sea. On this and later journeys he discovered and explored the rivers Murray and Darling and their tributaries. He found that these rivers did not flow into an inland sea at all but entered the ocean near the settlement of Adelaide. On these journeys the party met with terrible hardships. At times the only water they could get was squeezed out of mud from the bottom of dried-up pools. So great were their troubles that Sturt's health suffered: he became partly blind and had to leave the army.

But as soon as he was fit again, he set out on another journey to find the inland sea. This time he was quite sure that he would use his boat, because a party led by Edward Eyre had discovered a great salt lake which was named after him. On this second journey Sturt and his men met with even greater troubles. 'The ground was so hot', he wrote, 'that the dogs lost the skin off their paws. The men had their backs blistered and their shoes were burnt as if by fire.' They did not find any inland sea; only sand dunes and stony desert as far as they could see. Sturt sent some

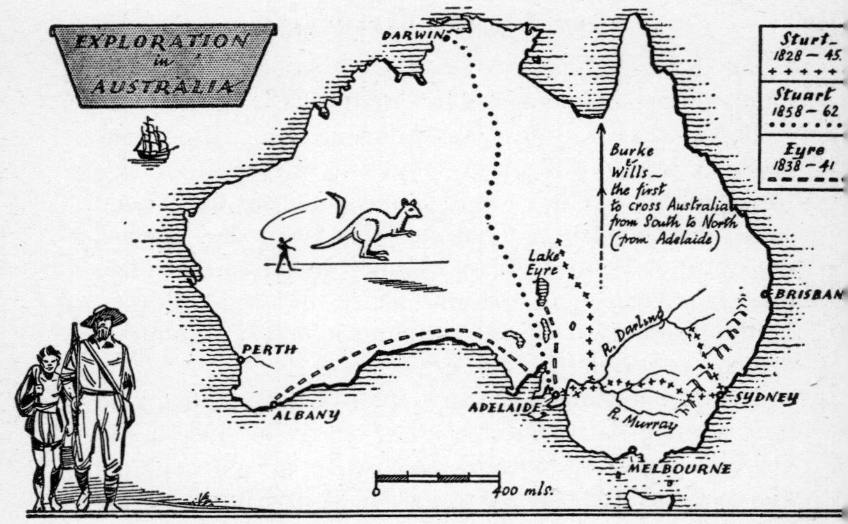

men home and made a desperate effort to push on, but in vain. They returned to Adelaide after more than a year and a half away. A few years later, Sturt went home to England—blind.

Then, just as Stanley carried on the work of Livingstone, so Sturt's work was continued by a man who had accompanied him on the last expedition. This was John McDouall Stuart, born at Dysart in Fife, who made six journeys into the interior. He finally proved that there was no inland sea after all, and that much of central Australia is hot, dry desert. His last journey in 1862 was right across the continent to Darwin. His party was not the first to cross Australia from north to south, however: a party under Robert Burke and W. J. Wills had done so a few months before, but both perished on the return journey. Such is the price men have paid for our knowledge.

The Arctic and the Antarctic

During the nineteenth century there were several expeditions to explore the polar regions. For example, by 1850 Admiral Sir John Ross, who belonged to Inch in Wigtownshire, had made three journeys to the Antarctic; and the Ross Sea is named after him. But the difficulties were great: the North Pole is surrounded by frozen sea, the South Pole by frozen land, and in both regions it is dark for six months of the year.

The North Pole was the first to be reached. In 1895 Dr. Nansen, a Norwegian, took his ship *Fram* as far through the ice as he dared to go. Then he began the long journey across the ice on dog-sledge. But his food supplies ran short and he had to turn back when he had less than 250 miles to go. In 1909 the Pole was reached by Commander Peary, an American. He left his ship *Roosevelt* at Cape Columbia and reached the North Pole after thirty-seven days' journey over the ice.

Already in the years 1901–1904 a British expedition had sailed south to the Antarctic under the command of Captain Robert Scott. This was the voyage of the famous *Discovery*. Lieutenant Ernest Shackleton joined the party but had to return home. In 1908, however, he led an expedition and reached a point less than a hundred miles from the South Pole.

Then, after Peary had reached the North Pole, the race for the South Pole began. Britain, Norway, Germany and Japan all organised expeditions: the British one was led by Captain Scott (see Plate 8), the Norwegian by Roald Amundsen. Probably you have read about the last stage of

Scott's journey with his four companions: Dr. Wilson, Captain Oates, Lieutenant Bowers and Petty Officer Evans.

Day after day they trudged over the snow and the ice, the men themselves pulling the sledges. When they knew they were only a few miles from the South Pole, they came across tracks. In January 1912 they found a tent and discovered that Amundsen's party had arrived there less than a month before. As Scott wrote in his diary, it was 'a terrible disappointment' after all their efforts.

On the journey back came disaster after disaster. Edgar Evans fell ill, struggled on bravely for almost a month, then collapsed and died. Oates was suffering from badly frostbitten feet and could hardly move. In vain he tried to persuade the others to leave him to die alone, but they refused. When they woke one morning a blizzard was blowing. Oates rose, painfully. 'I am just going outside', he murmured, 'and may be some time.' In order to give the others a chance to live, he walked out to his death. His sacrifice was in vain. Shortly afterwards, a raging blizzard kept Scott, Wilson and Bowers prisoners in their little tent. Food and fuel were finished, and they died, helpless from hunger, cold, and exhaustion.

Today there are still parts of the world largely unexplored and unknown to us. Little is known about some of the tribes of the Amazon basin in South America. Quite recently the Stone Age folk of the Central Highlands of New Guinea met white men for the first time. Mount Everest was not climbed until it was conquered in 1953 by Edmund Hillary and Sherpa Tenzing of Colonel John Hunt's party (see Plate 9). So man's knowledge of the world increases—but, as we have seen, this knowledge has been dearly bought.

THINGS TO DO

1. Make the following summary in your notebook:

Exploration in the 19th and 20th Centuries

Africa	*Australia*	*Arctic and Antarctic*
Livingstone	Sturt	Ross
Stanley	Eyre	Nansen
Mungo Park	Burke and Wills	Peary
		Shackleton
		Scott

2. Write a short note about the work of each of these men.

3. Write paragraphs on 'David Livingstone's work' and 'Scott's last exploration'.

4. The stories of these explorers are packed full of thrills and adventure. Try to read more about them.

5. On blank maps of Africa and Australia show, in different colours, the journeys we have read about.

6. On maps of Africa, Australia and the Polar regions you will find a great many places named after these explorers. Find as many as you can.

7. This is the last entry in Captain Scott's diary, which will give you some idea of their last few days. Copy it into your notebook and, as you write, imagine how *he* felt as he wrote it.

Thursday March 29.

Since the 21st we have had a continuous gale from W.S.W. and S.W. We had fuel to make two cups of tea apiece and bare food for two days on the 20th. Every day we have been ready to start for our depôt, eleven miles away, but outside the door of the tent it remains a scene of whirling drift. I do not think we can hope for any better things now. We shall stick it out to the end, but we are getting weaker of course, and the end cannot be far.

It seems a pity, but I do not think I can write more.

R. Scott

20

The Work of Doctors

IMAGINE that you are a young worker more than a hundred years ago in one of the factories that have sprung up in Scotland and England.

One day in 1840 your hand has been caught in a machine and terribly injured. You are taken away to a hospital, a rather dirty, dull and smelly place. You are met, perhaps, by a 'nurse', an unkempt old woman, and taken to a doctor who looks more like a workman in his grubby and stained old coat. He looks at your hand, shakes his head sadly and says that as far as he can see there is nothing he can do to save it. You are taken to a smaller separate room, perhaps given a drink of spirits, and made to lie on a table. There and then, with nothing to deaden the pain, the surgeon amputates. Then your arm is bandaged and you are carried off to bed.

That is not the end of your troubles, for in a day or two it is clear that your arm is poisoned. The doctors do what they can, but a bad poisoning, called gangrene, has set in. However, let us look on the bright side and say that after long weeks of suffering you are able to go home. You are maimed and unable to do heavy work again, but you think yourself lucky. You might have died from the shock of the operation, or from the poisoning that followed it. Many people do.

But you have not been home many days before an epidemic of that dredead disease called cholera sweeps through the town. It caused many deaths in your street three years ago, so you sit at home, wondering if your family will be lucky this time.

It is not a pretty picture, is it? But it really was as bad as this. Something like this could easily have happened to a great many families in the Scotland your great-great-grandfather knew. Now just pause a minute to think what would happen to you today if you had a similar accident. It would all be very different, wouldn't it? Why? Because many brave men and women, doctors, scientists, nurses, have worked to make our lives longer, safer and healthier. The story begins a few years before 1800.

First of all men had to find out more about the body and how it works. This study is called 'anatomy'. A great deal of work was carried on at Edinburgh University. There are gruesome stories of 'body snatchers' who stole corpses from graveyards in the night. You may have heard of the terrible Burke and Hare who, before they were caught, made quite a business of killing people to supply to the unsuspecting doctors. In such ways more was learned about the working of the human body.

Next, it was necessary to find some way of reducing the pain and shock of an operation. If a way could be found to make the patient unconscious, surgeons would not have to hurry and would be able to do more delicate operations. Before 1800 Humphry Davy had discovered that if he breathed nitrous oxide, 'laughing gas', he became unconscious; and about 1840 an American dentist showed that ether had the same effect. A German doctor discovered chloroform and James Simpson, a native of Bathgate, began to use it for his operations in the hospital

AN OPERATION AT ABERDEEN IN LISTER'S DAY

(*Compare this drawing with Plate* 15)

at Edinburgh. Old-fashioned doctors tried to stop Simpson's new methods, but slowly his ideas were followed. One great danger of operations was ended.

But the second danger remained: infection and gangrene. A German, Robert Koch, and a Frenchman, Louis Pasteur, found that the trouble is caused by living things in the air so tiny that they cannot be seen by the naked eye.

These we call 'microbes', and they are the cause of many diseases.

A Glasgow surgeon, Joseph Lister, realised that wounds were infected by microbes in the air and on the hands and instruments of the surgeon. So Lister tried to kill them by using carbolic acid, which is still used as a disinfectant. His method was to have a spray in the operating-room which sprayed the area of the operation. The surgeon, patient and attendants were soaked and other doctors thought it a huge joke. But they were more serious when they saw that Lister's patients healed quickly and cleanly. The old, dirty, slipshod methods were at an end.

Koch and Pasteur went on to find out more about microbes. Koch, for example, found the microbe that causes the illness known as tuberculosis. Pasteur made the discovery that when a disease microbe attacks a person, the body begins to build a defence against it. Often that defence stays on to fight any future infection. This is why you usually catch things like mumps and measles only once.

After this discovery Pasteur went on to make more experiments. He began to breed specially weak disease microbes and never let them grow strong and dangerous. Then he gave injections which contained these weak microbes. As he expected, the microbes were too weak to do any real harm, but the body built up a defence just as if it was in danger—and the protection stayed on. So began the idea of inoculation. You may have heard how, years before, Edward Jenner had begun something similar: vaccination against smallpox.

About the middle of the nineteenth century doctors

began to use their three most important 'tools'. First came the stethoscope, then the clinical thermometer, and then the hypodermic syringe which was invented by Alexander Wood, an Edinburgh doctor.

All these changes meant that trained and skilled nurses were needed to replace the slovenly old women who had worked in hospitals before. Florence Nightingale, 'The Lady with the Lamp' to soldiers in the Crimean War,

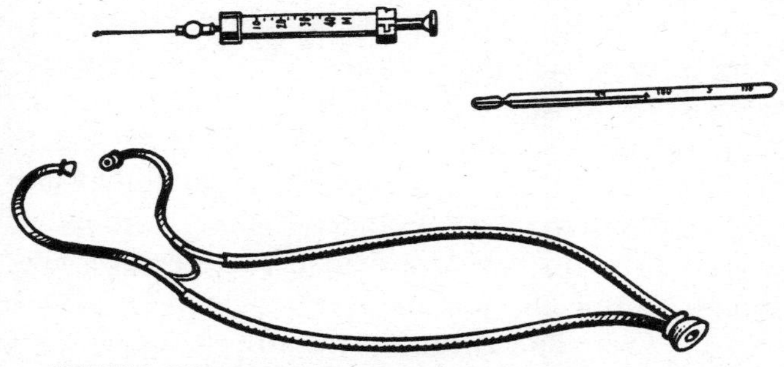

MEDICAL INSTRUMENTS: HYPODERMIC SYRINGE, CLINICAL THERMOMETER, STETHOSCOPE

began a school for nurses in London and did more than anyone else to improve the training of nurses.

Shortly before 1900 scientists made other great discoveries. The most widespread disease in tropical countries was malaria. Sir Ronald Ross discovered that the malaria microbe was carried by a certain kind of mosquito, which could be killed in its swampy breeding-places.

This was of great importance to folk in tropical lands, but the work of a German, Wilhelm Röntgen, will seem more important to you. He discovered that certain rays, which we now call X-rays, are able to pass through some substances such as wood which stop ordinary light rays. Photographs taken with X-rays show things inside these substances. Plates 13 and 14 show the usefulness of X-rays not only to doctors but to workers in industry too.

A third important discovery about this time was made by Mme. Marie Curie and her husband. Marie was a poor Polish student who went to Paris University and finally married a professor, Pierre Curie. Together they discovered a new substance, radium, which is used by doctors in the fight against diseases such as cancer.

And in this century the fight against disease goes on. The two World Wars gave surgeons and doctors many wounded and sick patients and they learned from their experience. In the last war a new drug came into use. It had been discovered by Alexander Fleming, a country lad from Loudoun in Ayrshire who became a professor in London. During the war more experiments were carried on by an Australian chemist, Howard Florey, at Oxford University. Probably you have guessed that this wonderful new drug was the one that has probably cured you at some time—penicillin. Perhaps you have heard of other drugs or 'antibiotics' such as 'M & B'. These initials stand for 'May and Baker', one of the many firms of manufacturers who make large quantities of these drugs for our use.

You may have heard as well about two modern kinds of vaccination. Two illnesses that doctors are fighting now are tuberculosis or 'TB' and poliomyelitis or 'polio'. You, and your brothers and sisters, will be given protection against these illnesses if your parents wish you to have it. The vaccination against tuberculosis is called

'BCG': the 'B' stands for 'bacillus' or germ (in this case a helpful one); the 'C' and 'G' stand for the names of the two Frenchmen who began experiments—Calmette and Guérin. One kind of 'polio' vaccination is called after Dr. Salk, the American doctor who first produced it.

* * *

Let us finish this chapter with two thoughts. First, think again how much safer, happier and healthier life is today than it was a hundred years ago. Secondly, notice how all this pioneer work was done in many countries by men and women of many nationalities. We are proud that Scotland and Scotsmen played their part, but we owe a great deal to Frenchmen, Germans, Americans, Poles—and many others too.

THINGS TO DO

1. Write a sentence about the work of each of the following people: Humphry Davy, James Simpson, Koch and Pasteur, Joseph Lister, Edward Jenner, Florence Nightingale, Ronald Ross, Wilhelm Röntgen, Marie and Pierre Curie, Alexander Fleming, Howard Florey.

2. Make sure that you understand the meaning of these words: anatomy, infection, inoculation, injection, vaccination, microbe, anaesthetic, X-ray, 'BCG'.

3. Why was there so much disease and ill-health in Scotland a hundred years ago? Try to find out more about the work your Town or County Council does to protect your health.

4. Try to read more about the life and work of at least one of these men and women.

21

The Work of Scientists

YOU have often heard people say that we live in a scientific age. But have you ever stopped to think just how much scientists have changed our world?

We have read about many scientists and inventors already. In chapter 20 we saw how many doctors and other scientists have made our lives healthier. Then there were the inventors who gave the world new forms of power. In the eighteenth century Newcomen and Watt showed the use of steam. In the nineteenth, Daimler experimented with the 'internal combustion' petrol-engine. In this century, Whittle in Britain and Heinkel in Germany made practical gas turbine or 'jet' engines. All these have speeded up travel and have helped men to produce goods quickly and cheaply.

But there were other wonderful discoveries that we have not mentioned at all so far. We have said nothing yet about the progress that has been made in physics and chemistry and mathematics, the subjects on which all other sciences are based.

The first real scientists and mathematicians in the world were the men of ancient Greece. Euclid was one; another was Archimedes, whose experiments you may have carried out yourself. From such men the scientists of the Renaissance learned to be more curious and to experiment to add to their knowledge. You know about Galileo the Italian, and other scientists who worked in other countries. In England William Harvey discovered how blood circulates in our bodies. Isaac Newton discovered the law of gravity and taught that there must be other 'laws' to explain how

A LABORATORY 400 YEARS AGO

things happen. In France Antoine Lavoisier and in Scotland Joseph Black of Edinburgh taught that accurate weighing and observation were necessary in all experiments.

Early in the nineteenth century John Dalton, an English chemist, did very important work. In Dalton's time men knew that some substances such as salt were 'compounds' of two or more things, which could be split up in the laboratory. Other substances, such as iron and copper, are single substances called 'elements'. Also, since the days of the ancient Greeks, men had guessed that these elements were made up of very tiny particles. Dalton called these particles 'atoms', and he carried out many experiments to find out more about them.

Dalton listed twenty elements: now we know over a hundred. Since his time we have learned a great deal about chemical elements and compounds, and today chemistry helps industry in countless ways. Scientists have shown how new materials can be made—such as 'synthetic' or artificial rubber, and 'plastic' materials such as nylon and terylene. Large new industries have grown up to make these things. Scientists have given farmers artificial fertilisers and chemical sprays which help farmers to grow more food. Finally, remember the drugs and antiseptics that scientists have given doctors as weapons in the war against ill health and disease.

* * *

It was not till Dalton's time, about 1800, that men seriously tried to find the secrets of the invisible power of electricity. The ancient Greeks, again, knew that if they rubbed a piece of amber it would pick up little pieces of straw or feathers—just as your fountain pen picks up little scraps of paper. Long afterwards, in Queen Elizabeth Tudor's reign, William Gilbert wrote about such substances which he called 'electrica', from *elektron*, the Greek word for amber.

About 1750 an American, Benjamin Franklin, tried to show that this magnetism or electricity was not just made by rubbing, but could be collected in various ways. He said, too, that lightning was a form of electricity. To prove this he sent up in a thunderstorm a kite with a metal rod sticking out of it. At the end of the string was a metal key. As he expected, the electricity from the thunder-clouds turned his key into a magnet and he was even able to set spirits on fire with it. (This experiment also gave him the idea of using lightning conductors to prevent buildings from damage.)

By 1800 experiments were being carried on in France, Italy, Germany, Sweden and Holland. In Italy, Luigi Galvani had some bodies of frogs in his laboratory for experiments. They were hanging on copper hooks and he noticed that they jerked when they touched an iron railing. So he began to experiment with these two metals, joining one to a frog's nerve and the other to a muscle. It gave the jerk he expected and he guessed that there was electricity in the frog's body. But another Italian, Alessandro Volta, showed that the electricity was the result of connecting the two different metals. He went on to make batteries by putting pieces of copper and zinc in weak acid. These were called, after him, 'voltaic' batteries. They are little used now, but of course we still measure electrical energy in volts.

Shortly after this Hans Oersted, a Dane, discovered a remarkable thing about the wire joining the copper and zinc in these batteries. If he held it above a compass needle the needle moved to one side. The same thing happened even when the battery was a long way from the compass. However long the wire, the compass needle could be moved to one side, and this led to the idea of sending signals by electricity. In 1837 Charles Wheatstone invented the electric 'needle' telegraph. (Telegraph comes from two Greek words meaning 'writing' and 'afar'.) Several needles were moved by electricity to point to letters on a board, and this meant that letters could be flashed very quickly from place to place. By 1860 cables had been laid across the English Channel and across the Atlantic. These long-distance telegraphs did not use needles but the system of dots and dashes which you know: the alphabet invented by the American, Samuel Morse.

One of the men who made the Atlantic telegraph possible was Lord Kelvin. The beginning of his career was his entry to Glasgow University at the age of ten! Twelve years later he became a professor; and he worked there for over fifty years. During that time he helped and encouraged many other scientists, and invented a great many instruments which were needed as electricity was put to many different uses. Another Scot whose work greatly helped other scientists was James Clerk Maxwell, who for a time was a professor at Aberdeen. He got some of his ideas from Lord Kelvin's writings, and his own discoveries and calculations made the work of later scientists possible.

Already a German named Reiss proved that electrical apparatus could be used to carry sounds which could be heard at a distance. In 1875 the telephone was invented by Alexander Graham Bell, a Scot who had gone to live in America. Also in America lived Thomas Edison, who made over a thousand inventions and had much to do with the first telephones, electric lamps, gramophones and moving pictures.

Even more astonishing than the early telegraphs and telephones was the coming of 'wire-less' telegraphy and 'radio' telephony: the sending of messages and speech without wires. A German, Hertz, picked out and measured wireless waves in 1888. Guglielmo Marconi, an Italian, came to work in England. A few years later he sent a message almost two miles; and after another five years he sent a message across the Atlantic. 'Wireless' had come, but the B.B.C. did not come into being until 1922. Ask your parents or grandparents to tell you about the 'cat's whisker' sets of the 1920's.

Later scientists were working on equipment which would enable things to be seen at a distance: in other words, television. The chief pioneer work here was carried out by a Scot, John Logie Baird, a native of Helensburgh. Much had to be done before it could be widely used and it was not until 1936 that the B.B.C. produced its first TV programme. In 1952 the programmes reached Scotland.

Another Scot, Sir Robert Watson-Watt, invented 'radar'. The radar set sends out wireless waves which are reflected by obstacles in their path. Radar is now commonly used in the navigation of aircraft.

Long before this men had discovered better ways of generating or making electricity. Michael Faraday, who began work as a bookbinder's apprentice, made the first electric motor driven by a battery. After ten years he produced a machine to make electricity, called a 'dynamo' (from the Greek word for power). The main part of the dynamo is a magnet round which coils of wire are turned by some form of power. Steam was generally used to turn the coils of the early dynamos, but in the great modern power houses this is often done by water power supplied by our 'hydro-electric' schemes. But scientists of the twentieth century have discovered another power to drive dynamos—atomic energy.

You remember that Dalton discovered that all materials are made up of atoms, which he believed could not be split up. But about 1900 J. J. Thomson and Lord Rutherford found that an atom is made up of a central part or core with other parts round it. Later, scientists discovered that in one kind of the metal uranium, which they called uranium 235, the centre of the atom can be split. When a lump of uranium is a certain size, millions of atoms can be exploded in a very short time, giving out so much heat that the temperature rises to millions of degrees centigrade. This is what happened when the first atomic bomb was dropped on the city of Hiroshima in 1945.

Today it is possible to control the splitting of the atoms so that the heat is not produced all at once, in a vast explosion, but in a steady controllable stream. Such heat can be used to make steam to drive some of the electric dynamos that supply the nation's electricity. The first atomic power station was opened at Calder Hall, Northumberland, in 1956. Today many more power stations are being added. One is working at Chapel Cross near Dumfries; another is being built at Hunterston near Ayr. At Dounreay, near Thurso, there is a big atomic research station, which also produces power (see Plates 18 and 19).

* * *

In this chapter we have found how many scientists have added to our knowledge, and how their skill has been used to improve men's lives. We hope that atomic energy, too, will be used to improve lives and not to destroy them.

THINGS TO DO

1. Write one sentence about the work of each of these men: John Dalton, Benjamin Franklin, Luigi Galvani, Alessandro Volta, Hans Oersted, Charles Wheatstone, Samuel Morse, Lord Kelvin, James Clerk Maxwell, Andrew Graham Bell, Thomas Edison, Guglielmo Marconi, John Logie Baird, Robert Watson-Watt, J. J. Thomson and Lord Rutherford.

2. Make a list of the ways in which chemistry has helped industry, farmers and doctors.

3. Try to find out more about the life of J. L. Baird and his experiments with TV.

4. Write down the meanings of these words and explain how they entered our language: magnet, electricity, galvanometer, galvanise, volt, ohm, watt, dynamo, ampere.

PARLIAMENT HOUSE, EDINBURGH

The house of the Parliament of Scotland until 1707

THE SCOTTISH REGALIA

Used at the crowning of kings

BUILDINGS IN THE NEW WORLD AND THE OLD

3. (*Above*) A model of Jamestown, Virginia, the first permanent English settlement in America, as it was in 1607

4. (*Below*) Louis XIV's palace at Versailles, near Paris

EDINBURGH—THE 'OLD TOWN' AND THE 'NEW TOWN'

5. (*Left*) Gladstone's Land, Lawnmarket 6. (*Right*) Charlotte Square

7. THE GENERAL ASSEMBLY OF THE CHURCH OF SCOTLAND
Held each year in the Assembly Hall, Edinburgh

8. ON THE WAY TO THE SOUTH POLE

Captain Scott, photographed in 1911

9. THE CONQUEST OF EVEREST

Tenzing at the summit, 1953

10. LOCOMOTIVES, OLD AND NEW. (*Above*) The Wylam Dilly Locomotive, 1813
(*Below*) A locomotive built at Glasgow for export to South Africa, 1957

11. MOTOR CARS, OLD AND NEW

(*Left*) Albion 1902

(*Below*) Jaguar 1958

12. AIRCRAFT, OLD AND NEW

(*Below*) The Wright Brothers' first flight, December 1903

12. AIRCRAFT, OLD AND NEW (*continued*)

(*Above*) The airship R 34

(*Left*) The Twin Pioneer, made at Prestwick by Scottish Aviation Ltd.

(*Below*) Comet jet airliner

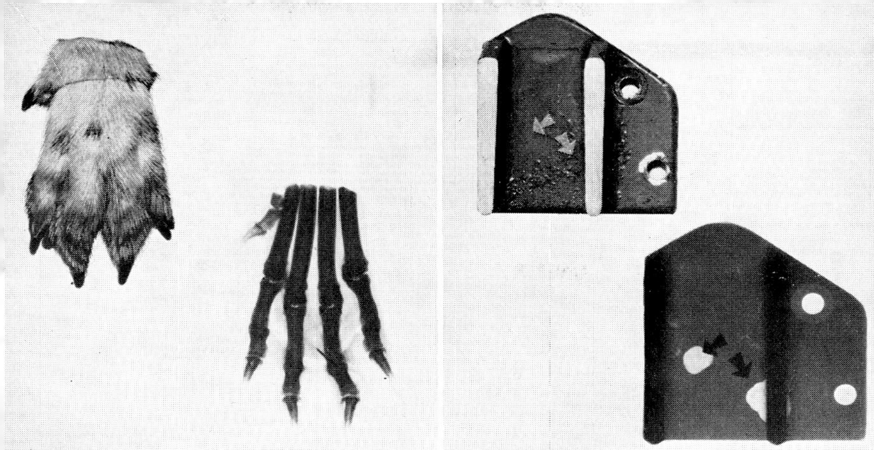

13. X-RAYS IN SURGERY: a needle in a dog's paw discovered by X-rays

14. X-RAYS IN INDUSTRY: faults in a casting revealed by X-rays

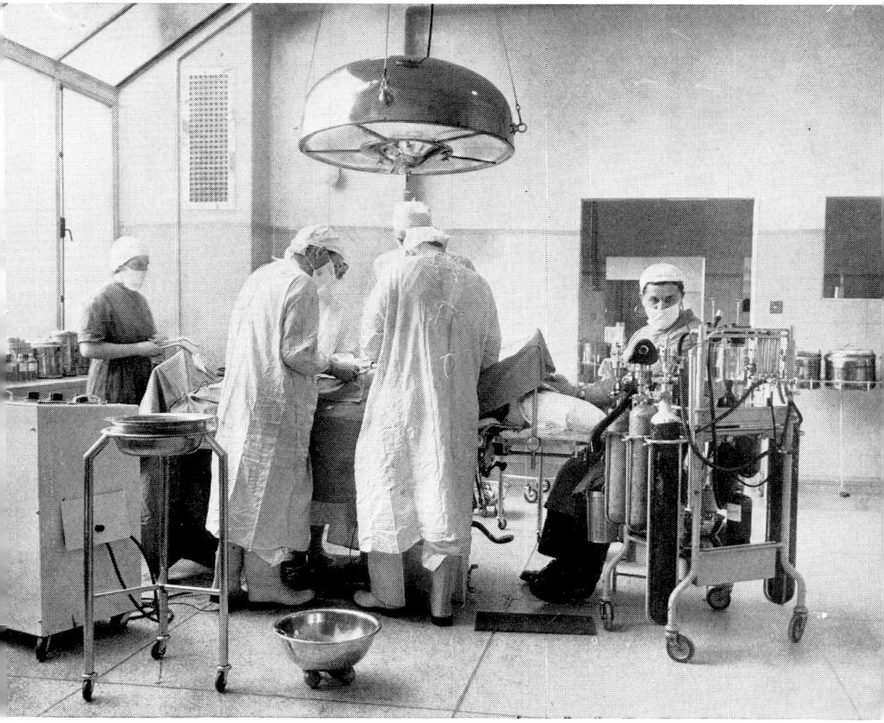

15. A MODERN OPERATING THEATRE: an operation in progress at Aberdeen Infirmary

16. A RESEARCH LABORATORY at the works of Thomas Hedley & Co. Ltd., Newcastle

17. THE RADIO TELESCOPE AT JODRELL BANK, CHESHIRE
Photographed at night while tracking a 'sputnik'

8. (*Above*) AN ATOMIC POWER STATION under construction at Dounreay, on the Caithness coast

9. A WORKER AT DOUNREAY. He wears protective clothing to shield him from harmful radioactivity

20. HEIL HITLER! The Führer being welcomed by the Reichstag in 1942

21. NAZI AND FASCIST LEADERS. Goering, Mussolini, Hess, Hitler, Himmler and Ciano (after the Munich Conference, 1938)

22. ALLIED LEADERS IN 1945
Churchill, Roosevelt and Stalin at Yalta, in the Crimea

23. DUNKIRK, 1940

The evacuation of British troops (*from a painting by Charles Cundall*)

24. (*Bottom, left*) THE BATTLE OF BRITAIN, 1940

R.A.F. fighter pilots running to take off in their Spitfires

25. (*Bottom, right*) THE RUSSIAN FRONT, 1941

German Panzers carrying infantry advancing against the Russians

26. THE WESTERN DESERT, 1942: Australian troops, under cover of a smoke screen, approaching a strong point

27. (*Above*) D-DAY, 1944
Troops assembling on the Normandy beach from landing craft in the background

28. (*Left*) THE COMMANDO MEMORIAL, INVERNESS-SHIRE
'The whole earth is the tomb of heroic men and their story is not written only on stone but abides everywhere woven into the stuff of other men's lives'

Part Three

WAR AND PEACE

22

The British Empire in 1914

IN BOOK ONE we saw that in Tudor times Englishmen were already interested in lands overseas. Although they did not know it, they were laying the foundations of an empire which straddled the world two centuries later.

In 1497 John Cabot discovered Newfoundland for Henry VII and this later became the first English colony. In the reign of Elizabeth, Sir Walter Raleigh tried to begin the colony of Virginia in North America. Early in the seventeenth century the East India Company began to trade with India and later ruled most of that vast country. About the same time the Hudson Bay Company was setting up trade in North America.

England became interested in colonies long after Spain and Portugal, but about the same time as France. You will remember what happened—French and British fought for India and for Canada in the long Seven Years War. The troops of the East India Company under Clive won most of India and the Company continued to rule it. The British army, including the new Highland regiments, won Canada from the French. But by this time the colonists in New England were ready to govern themselves. When the British government would not let them do so, they broke away, and the U.S.A. was born in 1783.

This was the end of one empire; but Britain gradually learned that she must find new ways of dealing with her colonies. So there began a new empire which was going to grow and change until it became the 'Commonwealth' we know today.

Canada

Canada was the first colony which Britain treated in a new way. There were troubles there in 1837—just as there had been troubles in New England more than fifty years before. But this time the British government did not merely send out troops—it sent out a statesman, Lord Durham, to see how things could be put right. As a result, the people of Quebec and Ontario were allowed to look after their own affairs. A Parliament like that of Britain was set up, and a Governor-General appointed by the Queen represented the Crown.

One of the greatest of the Governor-Generals was a Scot, Lord Elgin, who held the position from 1847 to 1854. He encouraged the growth of parliamentary government, and paved the way for the great events of 1867. In that year Quebec, Ontario, New Brunswick and Nova Scotia joined together to form the 'Dominion of Canada'. This

Dominion was a new nation, an 'offspring' of the Mother Country. It grew rapidly in size, wealth and freedom. By 1914 its territories stretched from coast to coast; and binding them together with a chain of steel was the Canadian Pacific Railway, completed in 1885, stretching 3,300 miles from Halifax in Nova Scotia to Vancouver in British Columbia.

Australia and New Zealand

We have already seen how the continent of Australia was explored: how Captain Cook mapped the coast and how Sturt, Stuart and other explorers found out more about the deserts of the interior. About 1850 the chief settlements were round the coast at Sydney, Melbourne, Adelaide, Perth and Hobart. These towns are among the

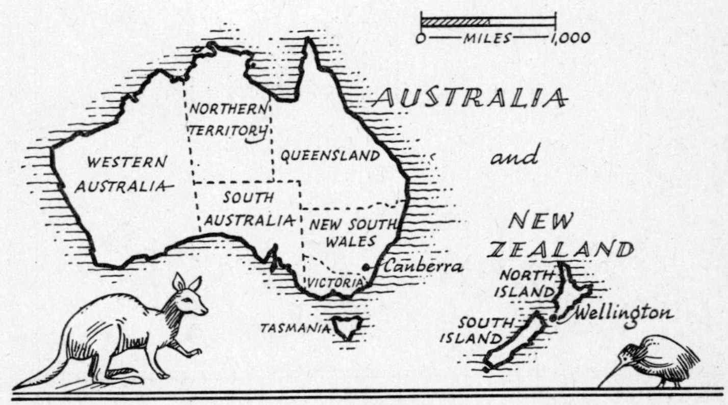

capitals of the six states of Australia. By this time settlers had realised that the lands of the south-east made good sheep pastures, and gold was discovered in Victoria in 1851.

From then on the population grew by leaps and bounds. Australia became rich and in 1901 she became a Dominion like Canada, with her own government looking after her own affairs. New Zealand, a thousand miles from Australia, had also been 'growing up' to a self-governing nation; and in 1907 she also was given the title of 'Dominion'.

South Africa

The fourth colony, or group of colonies, to be made a Dominion was South Africa, which was formed out of the four colonies of Cape of Good Hope (or Cape Colony),

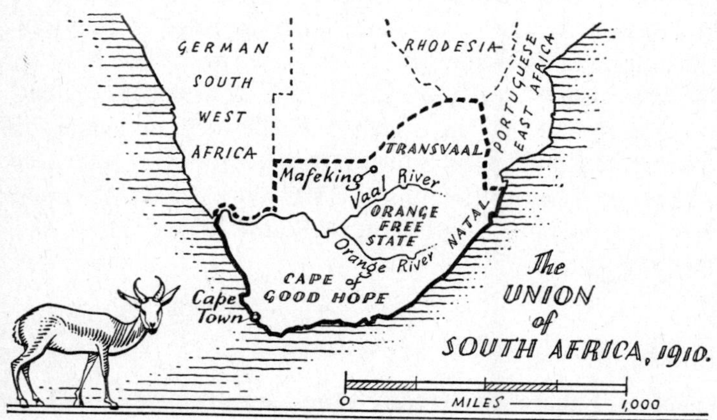

Orange Free State, Natal and Transvaal. Cape Colony passed from Holland to Britain at the end of the Napoleonic War. Naturally, the Dutch farmers (or Boers) did not like British rule—especially when the British government forbade them to keep slaves. So many of these Boers made a 'Great Trek' northward. With their covered wagons drawn by oxen they went in thousands across the Orange and Vaal rivers to set up the Orange Free State and Transvaal republics away from British rule. We will read more in Book 3 about the two wars between British and Boers. Perhaps you have heard of one of the events of these Boer Wars, of the siege of the town of Mafeking and its defence by Lord Baden-Powell.

Wars often breed bitterness and hatred; but after the Second Boer War ended in 1902, Britain did her best to make a lasting peace. The Boer republics came under the British Crown; but their peoples were granted three million pounds to rebuild their homes and buy seed and farm tools, and within a few years they were granted some self-government. Two men who had led the Boers in war, General Smuts and General Botha, now began to lead them in times of peace. They worked hard to persuade the four separate parts of South Africa to join into one free and self-governing Dominion. Their efforts were crowned with success, and the 'Union of South Africa' came into being in 1910.

West and East Africa

In 1914 there were many other important colonies in other parts of Africa. English traders, and those from other nations, were first interested in West Africa because they could get slaves there. This was how the English colony of Gambia began in the sixteenth century. In the Gold Coast (now known as Ghana) traders of many nationalities bought slaves as well as gold, but after the slave trade was abolished in 1807 the territory became British. Sierra Leone began about this time as a settlement where freed slaves could live and the chief town was named Freetown. The last and largest of the four British colonies in West

Africa in 1914 was Nigeria, where traders had followed the discoveries of Mungo Park.

We have already read about the discoveries of Mungo Park and David Livingstone. After Livingstone's death the countries of Europe realised how important these lands of Africa were and they began to grab them for themselves. In this 'Grab for Africa' Britain gained Rhodesia, British

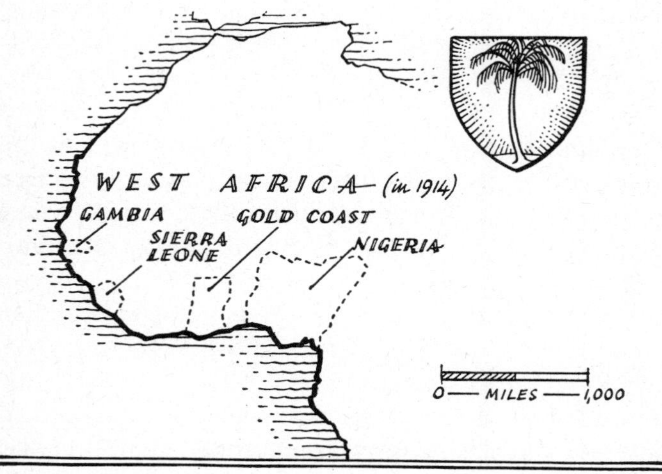

East Africa and parts of Somaliland and Eritrea. South of Egypt the great lands of the Sudan were won by a joint British-Egyptian army after the battle of Omdurman in 1898. They were ruled jointly by Britain and Egypt until 1955, when the Sudan became independent. Make sure that you know where these lands are.

In addition to ruling her African colonies, Britain was the governor of Egypt for forty years, up to 1922. In 1882 the Egyptian government was bankrupt and the Suez Canal, so important for trade with India and Australia, seemed to be in danger. A British 'adviser', supported by troops, was therefore sent out to make sure that Egypt was run in an orderly and efficient manner. In the years before 1914 Britain did good work in Egypt and the Sudan, building roads, railways and the great Aswan Dam on the Nile, and trying to improve the lot of the poor *fellahin* or peasants.

India

The early British colonies in India were ruled by the East India Company. But after 1784 they were ruled by a Governor-General appointed by the British government and the Company. During the rule of these Governors-General in the nineteenth century many important changes were carried out. Crime was put down and law and order enforced. Cruel customs were stopped—such as child-murder and *suttee* (the burning alive of a dead man's widow on her husband's funeral pyre). Roads and railways were built, water supplies were improved, postal services begun, schools and colleges were opened. The battle against famine and disease and ignorance was on.

But you can imagine that many Indians did not like these changes. Among many of the Indian soldiers, the *sepoys*, there was discontent which led to the Indian Mutiny of 1857. Peace was restored in the next year and, as we have seen, the British government took over the rule of the country from the East India Company altogether. Nearly twenty years later Queen Victoria was proclaimed

Empress of India, and she was represented by a Viceroy in place of the old Governor-General.

From that time more and more Indians demanded that they should be allowed to govern themselves. Britain did allow Indians to take a greater part in running their own

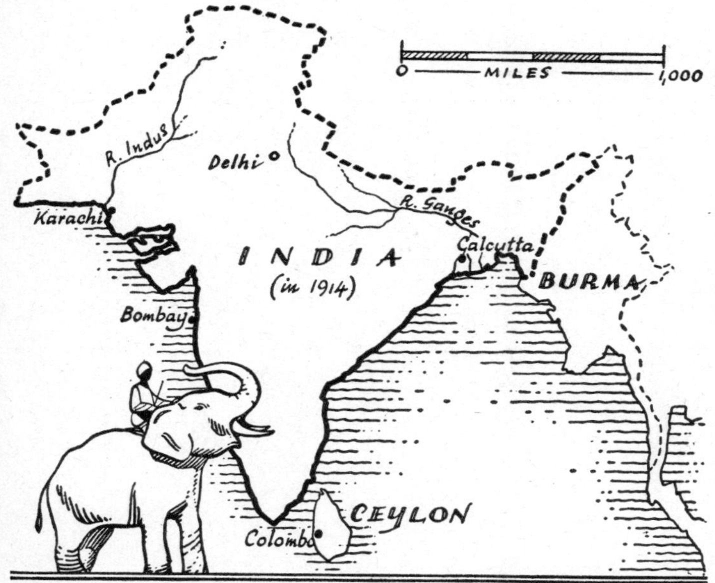

affairs, but by the time war broke out in 1914 they wanted to have complete control like other Dominions such as Canada.

* * *

So in 1914 Britain was at the head of a world-wide Empire. Most of it was contented, but in India, particularly,

SUBJECTS
of
KING GEORGE V.

there were problems to be settled. However, we can honestly say that Britain was a good ruler of her colonies and tried to make them better places to live in. All the peoples of the Empire rallied to the side of Britain when she was in danger in 1914.

THINGS TO DO

1. Make a set of maps of the parts of the Commonwealth we have read about. On them mark all the places mentioned in this chapter.

2. If you have not time to do all the maps, study an atlas carefully and make sure you know where all the places are.

3. Make sure of the meanings of these: Boer, the 'Grab for Africa', *fellahin*, *suttee*, *sepoy*, Viceroy.

4. Try to find out more about:

   (*a*) The building of the Canadian Pacific Railway;
   (*b*) The 'Gold Rush' in Australia;
   (*c*) The Great Trek;
   (*d*) The siege of Mafeking and Lord Baden-Powell;
   (*e*) The building of the Suez Canal;
   (*f*) The fighting at Cawnpore and Lucknow during the Indian Mutiny.

5. *Class work.* Try to make a collection of postage stamps from the lands of the Empire before 1914. Mount each country's stamps on a sheet of white paper and make a class display.

23

The First World War

IN THE next book we will learn a good deal more about Europe in the past hundred years. For the moment we will just look very quickly at those events which brought about the first great war in 1914.

Since 1815 there had been no war involving the whole of Europe. Nevertheless, wars and revolutions had altered the map of Europe very much. In Germany the many small states had been united into one country, mainly by the Prussian leader Bismarck. In 1870 Germany had defeated France in a short war and taken Alsace and Lorraine from her. Italy, like Germany, had become a united nation instead of a collection of little states. As a result, the Austrian empire had lost its lands in northern Italy, but by the early 1900's Austria was gaining new lands in the Balkans, where the Turkish empire was breaking up. Russia also was eager to gain parts of the Turkish empire and to protect the small countries—particularly Bulgaria and Serbia—which had been formed out of the old Turkish empire.

In 1914 the great countries of Europe were divided into two 'camps', each bound together by treaties. Germany and Austria were allies; and on the other side, so were Russia and France. For years, suspicion and fear had been growing between the two sides. Many British people feared Germany, because her ruler, the Kaiser, appeared to be so warlike and because the German navy had become so large and powerful. Then in the summer of 1914 the heir to the Austrian empire was murdered by a Serb at Sarajevo. The Austrians threatened to go to war with Serbia (part of what is now Yugoslavia); Russia began to mobilise her armies to help Serbia; Germany came to the help of Austria, and France came to the help of Russia. So when the war started we had this arrangement:

Serbia Russia France	*versus*	Austria Germany

and most of the other lands of Europe were soon to join in.

The German plan to win the war was simple, for they were sure that it would be a long time before the Russian armies would be ready to fight. So they left only a few troops on the eastern frontier and sent their great armies against France. They hoped to conquer France quickly and then deal with Russia.

* * *

The German armies marched through little Belgium, in spite of the brave resistance led by King Albert. Britain and other countries had promised to help Belgium if she were attacked, and so this brought Britain into the war. The German armies swept on towards Paris but were stopped at the great battle of the Marne. They were pushed back just beyond the River Aisne and there they dug trenches from which they could fight. The French and British armies did the same, and for four long years the two sides faced each other across an empty 'no man's land'.

You have probably heard of the horrors of this trench

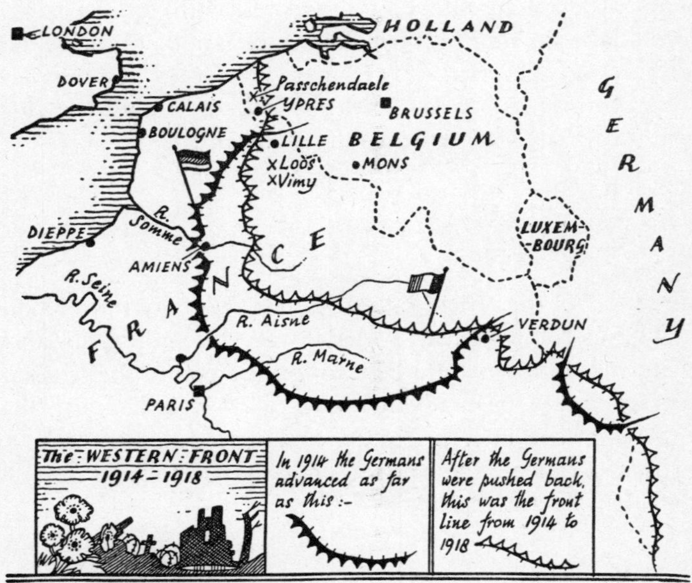

warfare and of the terrible battles which killed hundreds of thousands of men and turned 'no man's land' into a nightmare land of barbed-wire and shell-holes and broken buildings. The battles of this war were not like battles of the past, over in a few hours or a day or two: they dragged on for months and months. The battle of the Somme was fought for five months in 1916, from early July to late

November. The British forces, commanded by Sir Douglas Haig, tried to push the German army back. Great 'improvements' in weapons, especially in machine-guns and high-explosive shells, increased the casualties; and on the first day German machine-guns killed or wounded sixty

STAND-TO!

thousand men. Altogether there were half a million casualties in the French and British armies in this one drawn-out battle.

Both sides started using new weapons to try to bring the war to an end. The Germans used poison gas, the Allies invented 'tanks'. The Germans used airships called Zeppelins and both sides began to use aircraft for spotting, air-fighting and bombing. London was bombed, and this new form of attack was very frightening, although the raids were tiny compared with those of the Second World War.

There was little fighting between the battleships of Britain and Germany. Even in the battle of Jutland in 1916, Admiral Jellicoe and the German admiral were careful not

BOY CORNWELL, V.C., AT THE BATTLE OF JUTLAND

to risk their fleets too much. For by this time the Germans had decided to try to end the war quickly on the sea since they could not end it quickly on land. They built submarines, known as U-boats, hoping to starve Britain into surrender by sinking merchant ships bringing food and supplies. They nearly succeeded: in the month of April 1917 over four hundred ships were sunk.

But in the long run the U-boat campaign was unwise, for it was this that made America decide to enter the war on the side of the Allies. The U-boats were defeated by the help of the American navy; by grouping the ships in convoys protected by warships; and by new weapons such as the depth charge.

The year 1917 was important for another reason. Russian armies fought the German troops on the eastern front most bravely although they were badly armed, sometimes possessing only one rifle between three soldiers. The Czar's government had never been well organised: now it was overthrown by a revolution and the revolutionary government made peace with Germany. (You will read more about this in the next chapter.) Now Germany could concentrate all her forces on the Western Front.

There had been much fighting elsewhere, though on a smaller scale. In 1915, after the Turks sided with Germany, the Allies tried to capture Constantinople so that ships could move between Russia and western Europe. Thousands of troops, many of them from Australia and New Zealand, were landed at Gallipoli. They fought most gallantly, but the attack was a failure. In 1917, however, the Turkish possessions in Mesopotamia and Palestine were conquered and General Allenby entered Jerusalem. Allenby's forces had been helped by T. E. Lawrence, 'Lawrence of Arabia', who led tribesmen against their Turkish rulers.

Meanwhile fighting flared up again on the Western Front. The German armies retreated to a very strong line of fortifications called the 'Hindenburg Line'. The French attacked and suffered terrible casualties. In an attempt to help them, the British attacked too; and at Passchendaele, one of the most awful battles of the war, they lost three hundred thousand men.

Germany and her allies seemed to be in a very strong position in the spring of 1918. Her chief planner, General Ludendorff, decided to make a great effort to capture the

Channel ports of France. But new men were in charge on the Allies' side. Lloyd George, the Prime Minister of Britain, and Clemenceau ('The Tiger') of France spurred on their countrymen. Field-Marshal Haig was the British commander-in-chief, and the Allied forces on the Western Front were put under the command of one man —the French Marshal Foch.

On March 21st, 1918, came the greatest German attack

of all the war. The whole of the British Fifth Army was pushed out of the way. But the German troops never crossed the River Marne, and the British counter-attacked. By this time over a quarter of a million American soldiers had landed in France and these helped to turn the scale.

In the north, the German armies were actually pushed over the Hindenburg Line into Germany.

The armies of Germany were not finally defeated, but things looked hopeless for her. Her ports were blocked and her allies beaten: the Turks in Palestine, the Austrians in Italy. The German people lost hope, they rebelled against the government that had led them to disaster, and the Kaiser fled to Holland. At 11 a.m. on November 11th,

1918, the guns stopped firing and men laid down their arms.

Everyone was glad the killing was over, and everyone was agreed that it must never happen again. While it was being fought, this war had often been described as 'a war to end war'. But how was war to be prevented again? The leaders of the Allies met at Versailles. Of these leaders the most important were the 'Big Four': Lloyd George from Britain, Clemenceau from France, Orlando from Italy, and President Wilson of the United States.

At Versailles the victorious allies blamed Germany for starting the war. Her colonies were taken away from her; she was ordered to pay large sums of money to the Allies; her army and navy were made very small; and she lost valuable lands to other countries. Some of these lands Germany had taken years before (such as Alsace-Lorraine and part of Poland), but she also lost for a time the rich coalfields of the Saar valley. In years to come ordinary Germans felt that they had been unfairly treated, and asked why they should go on paying for the unwise acts of the ex-Kaiser and his generals.

Outside Germany, too, tremendous changes were made. The old Austrian empire came to an end, and from its vast territories were carved out a tiny Austrian republic and the new states of Czechoslovakia and Hungary. Yugoslavia and Poland, new states created by the peacemakers, also had large pieces of former Austrian territory, as did Rumania. The little Baltic countries of Estonia, Latvia, and Lithuania, which had been yielded by Russia to Germany in 1917, were allowed to remain in existence as independent states. Finland also became a separate state.

So after 1919 the map of Europe was dotted with new and almost unpronounceable names; stamp collectors had to stick new pages in their albums, and the old atlases were useless. Who caused all this re-drawing of frontiers and setting up of new nations? It was the work, above all, of the American President, Woodrow Wilson. He was determined that if possible none of the peoples of Europe should have to live under 'foreign' rule. So Czechoslovakia was made for the Czechs and Slovaks to live in, Hungary for the Hungarians, and so on. Wilson succeeded so well in his aim that only three per cent of the peoples of Europe were left under foreign rulers. These changes, and also some that took place in the countries of the Middle East (Syria, Palestine, Iraq and Egypt, for example) can be seen on the map on page 191.

Wilson had one other great idea, and he insisted that it should be made part of the peace treaty. This idea was that the nations of the world should band together in a league and promise to settle any disputes peacefully instead of by war. So the League of Nations was born and big headquarters were built at Geneva. Everybody hoped that this was the beginning of a great period of peace for the world.

THINGS TO DO

1. Write one sentence about each of these men, to show the part they played in the war or the making of the peace: Field-Marshal Haig, Admiral Jellicoe, General Ludendorff, Marshal Foch, Lord Allenby, Lawrence of Arabia, Lloyd George, Clemenceau, President Wilson.

2. Explain what is meant by Zeppelin, 'No man's land', trench warfare.

3. Write a paragraph about each of the following: the Gallipoli campaign; new weapons on land and in the air; the U-boat campaign.

4. What were the main changes made by the peace-makers at Versailles? Do you think Germany was harshly treated?

5. If you know someone who took part in the First World War ask him to tell you about it.

6. Find out more about the League of Nations. What else did it try to do besides keep peace?

24

The World after 1918

AFTER the war most people hoped that a new age of peace and happiness had begun. But many nations were not contented and were ready to listen to men who promised them power and wealth. They did not mind if they lost some of their freedom. As a result, in many countries there arose one man who was able to gather power into his own hands. Such a man, who was able to put out of the way anyone who opposed him, we call a 'dictator'. A 'dictatorship', as you can see, is the opposite of a 'democracy' where everyone is free to think and vote as he likes, without fear.

The twentieth century has seen many kings toppled down by revolutions and in many countries dictators have taken their place. In this chapter we will see what happened in Russia, Japan and China, Turkey, Italy and Germany.

Russia

We have already seen that there was a revolution in Russia even before the end of the war. The Russian people rebelled in 1917 because they blamed the Czar and his government for the defeats in battle—but they had been discontented for a long time. Even in the nineteenth century many Russians were serfs, no better than slaves, and were cruelly treated by their landlords. Even when the serfs were set free in 1861 the landlords kept so much of the land that the free peasants were desperately poor. One Czar, Alexander II, did try to improve their lot but changed his mind when there were several attempts to kill him. During the reign of the last Czar, Nicholas II, there were strikes and demonstrations which were harshly put down.

After 1905 a parliament called the *Duma* was set up, but few people had the vote and the Czar kept the real power in his own hands. So, as we have seen, he was blamed for the defeats after 1915. In 1917 the *Duma* was swept away and next year the Czar and his family were killed.

The leader of the revolutionists, the Bolsheviks, was a man who called himself Lenin. He was helped by Leon Trotsky and Joseph Stalin, 'the man of steel'. These men were 'Communists' who followed the teachings of a German, Karl Marx. This teaching was that all workers of the world should rebel against their rulers and unite. Then they could set up a dictatorship where the workers would have all the power. In Russia the new flag, the hammer and sickle, was designed to show that workers in factories and farms now had the power that had belonged to the Czar. But the real masters of Russia were now the few leaders of the Communist Party in the Kremlin palace in Moscow. Under their rule there were vast changes. 'Five Year Plans'—nation-wide

THE HAMMER AND SICKLE

programmes for the building up of industry and the improvement of agriculture—were announced and put into effect. Great new industrial towns, river dams to provide electric power and 'collective farms' run by the government sprang up. The people as a whole may not have liked all these rapid changes, but Russia did become a powerful modern state.

China and Japan

Great changes had begun before the war in China and Japan too. During the thirty years before 1900 Japan copied Western ideas and changed herself from a backward, isolated place into an up-to-date country with big industries. In 1905 she was strong enough to defeat the Russian fleet. But she had far too big a population for her small islands and she hoped for new lands for trade and settlers.

China looked an easy prey. In 1911 the last of the weak Manchu emperors was dethroned, and there followed years of civil war between groups of warlords. Slowly law and order was restored by Dr. Sun Yat-sen, who was followed by General Chiang Kai-shek. This powerful building up of the Chinese republic was stopped by the Japanese attack which we will read about in the next chapter.

Turkey

Another country which was most backward and had suffered under a weak ruler was Turkey. In 1923 the last Sultan was put off the throne and a republic was set up under President Kemal Ataturk. Ataturk was a dictator, but unlike the other dictators we are going to read about, he used his power only to improve the lives of his people, not to harm others. Against great opposition, he made Turkey 'westernise' itself. He introduced the alphabet we use, encouraged modern methods of agriculture, and forced his people to dress in European style. This one man was truly 'the maker of modern Turkey'.

Italy

Many Italians after the war were poor, hungry and restless, and many men were ready to listen to an ex-soldier named Benito Mussolini. He told them that Italy could find greatness again only if the whole nation gathered round a leader who had full power. As a badge for his party he chose the *fasces* of ancient Rome. This was a bundle of tightly bound rods with an axe: the sign of the ruler's powers in ancient Rome. Mussolini's followers were known as Fascists, or 'Blackshirts' from the uniform they wore.

FASCES

In 1922 Mussolini was strong enough to lead a march on Rome at the head of thirty thousand followers. He demanded control of the government and King Victor Emmanuel agreed. So Mussolini, now known as *Il Duce* or The Leader, made himself a dictator and punished or imprisoned anyone who opposed him. He kept the Italian Parliament in being, but all members had to be Fascists so it was completely under his control.

Germany

By this time there was a similar movement in Germany. The Germans hated the Treaty of Versailles, which they considered had punished them harshly, and were afraid of Communism. Many Germans, too, disliked the Jews who, they said, had too much wealth and power in Germany. They were ready to listen to the ideas of an ex-army corporal named Adolf Hitler, who became the leader of the little National-Socialist or Nazi party in 1919. Hitler, knowing how Germans loved military display, staged all kinds of parades and his followers wore a brown uniform with a swastika badge on the sleeve.

Things did not go well for Hitler at first and in 1923 he was imprisoned. In prison he wrote *Mein Kampf*, 'My Struggle', in which he set down what the Nazis wanted to do to make Germany great again. First, Hitler said that the 'punishment' Treaty of Versailles must be overthrown and Germany allowed to have her own army and navy again. Next, he said that the Germans were a great race but had been spoiled by Jews, who should be 'removed' from everyday life. Another part of Nazi teaching was that the Germans needed *lebensraum*, 'living-space', which must be gained by war if necessary.

SWASTIKA

In 1925 Field-Marshal Hindenburg, an honoured soldier, was elected President of Germany. He did not like Hitler at all, but during the next few years the membership of the Nazi Party grew and they won more and more seats in the German Parliament or *Reichstag*. This was a time of great unemployment when only the Nazi Party seemed to offer any hope to the many people who were hungry and out of work. In 1933 Hindenburg had to ask Hitler to be Prime Minister or Chancellor. A few weeks later a great

A CONCENTRATION CAMP

fire broke out in the Reichstag building and it was destroyed. Hitler immediately said the Communists were to blame and he persuaded President Hindenburg to give him special powers to arrest and imprison people without trial. You have probably heard the names of some of the prison-camps or 'concentration camps'—Belsen, Buchenwald and Dachau. Here prisoners whose only crime was disagreement with Hitler's ideas were horribly punished—

or killed. We should remember that concentration camps were first set up to punish the many Germans who opposed Hitler.

In 1934 Hindenburg died and Hitler made himself President as well as Chancellor. He called himself the *Führer*, the Leader, of Germany. Now he was in complete control and he gathered round him a group of men who remained the leaders of Germany till the end of the war. Goering, who loved to cover his big chest with medals, was the head of the *Luftwaffe*, the Air Force. Ribbentrop, who was the German Ambassador to Britain for a time, later became the Minister for Foreign Affairs. Goebbels was in charge of propaganda—the publishing of 'news', much of it twisted or invented to make Germans support the Nazi leaders. A ruthless man named Himmler controlled the Secret State Police, the *Geheime Staatspolizei* or Gestapo. The Gestapo had spies everywhere and young children were even taught to spy at home and tell their teachers what they heard their parents say. Some of the teachers, of course, were in touch with the Gestapo.

This was what the Germany of 1938 was like. Books which did not agree with Nazi teaching were publicly burnt. Jewish shops had *Jude*, Jew, scrawled over the windows. Jews and other opponents of Hitler were carried off to concentration camps to die or to live a life which was not worth living. Even past friends of Hitler were not safe if he suspected them. During the night of June 30th, 1934, several important Nazi leaders were taken from their homes and families and quietly murdered. This was the first of several 'purges'.

Britain and the other countries looked on, horrified but

helpless—for what the ruler of Germany did to the people of Germany seemed to be their business, not ours. But from 1934 onwards Hitler began to bully other peoples and this led to the Second World War. We will read about that in the next chapter. Meanwhile, read over all this again and try to realise what it was like to live under a dictator such as Hitler.

THINGS TO DO

1 Make sure you know the meaning of the following: dictator, *Duma*, *fasces*, *Il Duce*, Nazi, *Mein Kampf*, *lebensraum*, *Reichstag*, concentration camp, *Führer*, *Luftwaffe*, propaganda, Gestapo, 'purge'.

2. Write a brief note on each of the following: Alexander II, Nicholas II, Lenin, Trotsky and Stalin, Karl Marx, Dr. Sun Yat-sen and General Chiang Kai-shek, Kemal Ataturk, Field-Marshal Hindenburg, Goering, Ribbentrop, Goebbels, Himmler.

3. What things happened in Nazi Germany that you would not like to see happening in Scotland?

4. Read more about the lives and ideas of Karl Marx, Lenin, Mussolini, Hitler, Kemal Ataturk and Sun Yat-sen.

5. Both the Fascist and Nazi Parties paid great attention to training children and youths. See if you can discover anything about these youth organisations.

25

The Coming of the Second World War

In 1934, fifteen years after the Treaty of Versailles, to most people it did not seem possible that there could be another war. Italy under Mussolini supported the League of Nations, and in 1926 even Germany had been allowed to join. Japan was a member, too. Why should there be a war as long as there was a strong League of Nations to settle the world's problems?

But already events in the Far East had shown that the League was not strong enough to act when there was a danger of war. We saw in the last chapter that the Japanese government thought that Japan needed new lands for her big population to settle in, especially as Japanese settlers were not allowed to enter America, Canada or Australia. China seemed to be the obvious place, but she was growing stronger under General Chiang Kai-shek. However, in 1931 Japan, a member of the League of Nations, attacked China and the League did not stop her. Japan conquered the Chinese state of Manchuria and set up a government controlled from Japan. In 1937 Japan attacked China again and this Sino-Japanese War dragged on for eight years.

From 1931 onwards Mussolini had been watching what was happening. He saw how powerless the League was to stop an aggressor-nation and his ideas of a new Roman

Empire began to take shape. His eye had fallen on the kingdom of Abyssinia in East Africa, which lay between Italian Eritrea and Italian Somaliland. In 1935 he sent his armies into Abyssinia and they won easy victories over the poorly-armed Abyssinians. The Emperor of Abyssinia, Haile Selassie, went into exile and appealed to the League of Nations for help. The member-countries of the

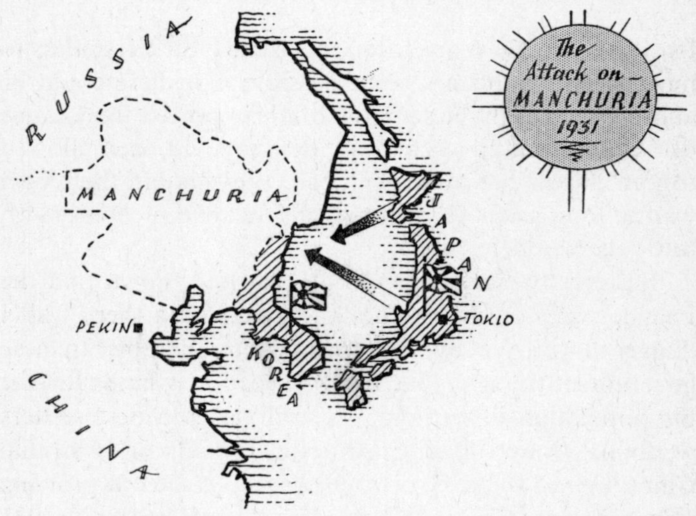

League decided to stop trading with Italy but this had little effect, and Abyssinia became part of the new 'Roman Empire'. So for a second time the League showed that it was too weak to stop a bully, and trade with Italy soon began again.

This 'punishment' of Italy by the League made the dictators of Italy and Germany work more closely together and their friendship came to be called the 'Rome–Berlin

Axis'. Now Hitler had seen how weak the League of Nations really was and he felt that he could be more daring. He showed this first in Spain.

King Alfonso XIII had given up the throne of Spain in 1931, and a republican government had been set up. Later a group of rebels led by General Franco were trying to defeat the government. Both Germany and Italy sent men

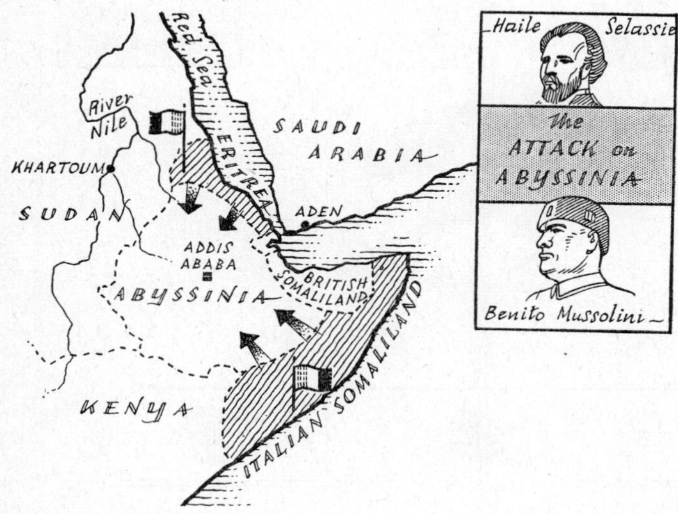

and arms to General Franco. Russia sent help to the Spanish government. Other countries such as Britain were not eager to help either side because they feared that this might be the beginning of another world war. But men of many nationalities fought against Franco's armies in the International Brigade. Franco did not win the quick victory he hoped for, but after three years' struggle he found himself the leader of a poor, broken, country.

Hitler had helped Franco to victory but he was not really very interested in Spain. He wanted to make a Greater *Reich*, a Greater German Empire. He took the first step in 1938 when he sent his troops into Austria and told the world that it was now part of Germany. This was known as the *Anschluss* or Union. It was only a first step, for Hitler

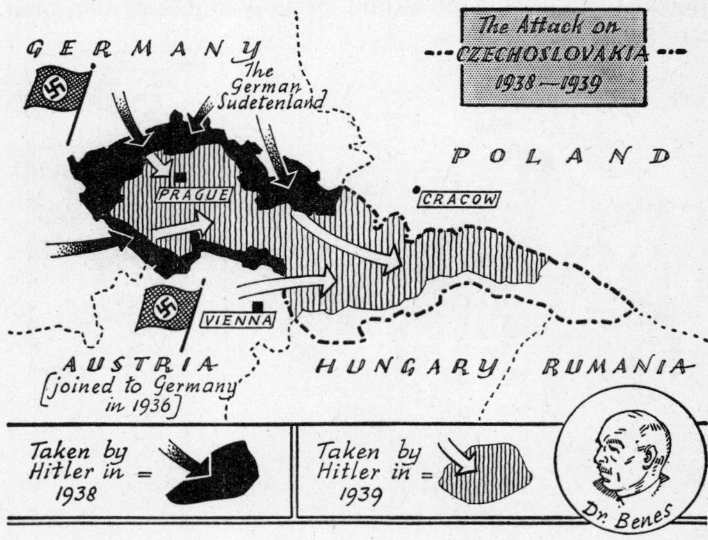

said he wanted to bring into the *Reich* those parts of other countries where most of the people were Germans. Soon afterwards he said he wanted the *Sudetenland*, the southern land, that part of Czechoslovakia which bordered on Germany. But the Czechs were not going to give up the *Sudetenland* without a struggle, and they were led by their courageous President, Dr. Benes.

The Czechs looked to France and Britain to support

them but they were disappointed, for the leaders of these two countries wanted to avoid war at all costs. Anyway, the people of the *Sudetenland* were of German blood, and many of them did want to be joined to Germany. It looked as if Hitler was ready to go to war, and in September 1938 Neville Chamberlain, the British Prime Minister, flew to meet Hitler to persuade him to keep the peace. At the Munich Conference, Britain, France and Italy agreed that

GERMAN TANKS ON THE MOVE

the *Sudetenland* should be given to Germany. In return, Hitler promised that he was now satisfied and that he did not want any more lands.

Six months later he showed what his promise was worth. Without warning, his Nazi troops marched into the remainder of Czechoslovakia and added it to Germany. These peoples he now conquered were not Germans, and it was obvious that Hitler was simply out to conquer. No nation was safe.

Certainly Poland was not. Part of Poland was the 'Polish Corridor', a narrow strip of land reaching to the Baltic Sea. It divided East Prussia from the rest of Germany, and it was almost certain that Hitler would want it next. He did. He told the Poles that he wanted a wide 'road' across the Corridor, but they refused—even though they knew what it meant to refuse. By this time France

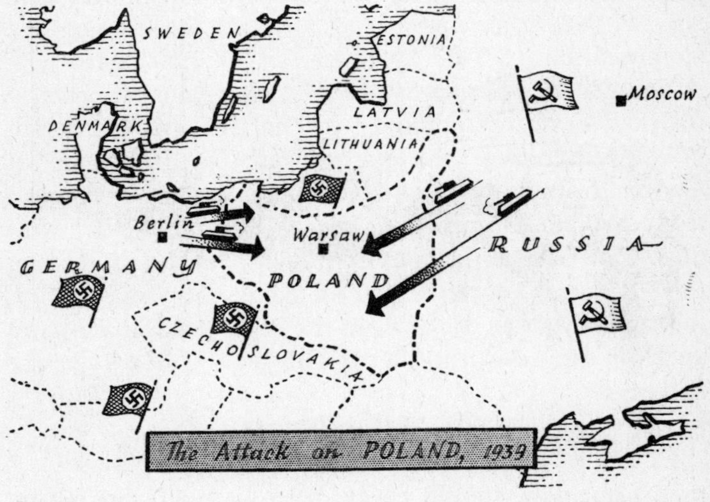

The Attack on POLAND, 1939

and Britain realised that Hitler must be stopped, even at the risk of war, and they promised to help Poland if Germany attacked her.

The summer of 1939 was a dreadful one, for every day seemed to bring war nearer. Obviously Hitler meant to attack Poland, for he put out false news about the ill-treatment of Germans living in Poland. Britain and France saw that they would need the help of Russia, Poland's neighbour, if Poland was to be saved. So they sent representatives to Moscow to try to persuade Stalin to join them in stopping Hitler. The talks went on and on for weeks. Meanwhile Hitler had sent his Foreign Minister, Ribbentrop, to try to persuade Stalin not to go to the help of Poland. Hitler won, and on August 23rd Stalin and Ribbentrop signed a treaty in which Germany and Russia promised not to attack one another. It was astonishing to see the Nazis making friends with their enemies, the Communists.

The world could hardly believe what had happened—for now there was nothing to stop Hitler marching into Poland. There was not long to wait. On September 1st German troops attacked Poland, and Warsaw was bombed from the air. Britain and France demanded the withdrawal of German troops from Poland. Hitler, of course, refused and we declared war on September 3rd.

On that Sunday the air-raid sirens sounded in Scotland and folk went down to their bomb shelters. Another war had begun.

THINGS TO DO

1. Explain, in your own words, how Japan, Italy and Germany tried to get more land and power for themselves.

2. Explain what the following mean: The 'Axis', the International Brigade, the *Anschluss*, the Polish Corridor.

3. Write a sentence on each of the following: Haile Selassie, Alfonso XIII, General Franco, Dr. Benes, Neville Chamberlain.

4. Do you think that Great Britain and France were right in declaring war on Hitler's Germany? Why?

26

The Second World War

LESS than three weeks after Hitler's soldiers marched into Poland, that unhappy country was defeated. The idea behind the treaty between Hitler and Stalin was seen now, because Russian troops marched into east Poland and the two dictators divided the country between them.

The fighting in Poland had shown the world the Nazi idea of *blitzkrieg*, 'lightning war'. In the west, however, it looked as if there might be the kind of fighting seen in the First World War: not from trenches this time, but from strongly fortified walls. The French army on the 'Maginot Line' faced the Germans standing ready in the 'Siegfried Line'. There was little fighting, but at home the British people made ready to meet the big air attacks they expected. Policemen, firemen, air raid wardens, ambulance men and women, were all organised in the 'Civil Defence Service'. 'Air Raid Precautions' (A.R.P.) were made: street lights were not lit and windows were blacked out. Men from 18 to 40 were called up for the Services if they were not in jobs where they were actually helping to win the war. Everyone was given an identity card, a gas mask and a ration book.

This 'phoney war' (as the Americans called it) ended in April 1940. Then Hitler attacked again. The victims this time were small countries who had not even declared war on him but hoped to remain neutral: Norway and Denmark. Within two months both were beaten. The British army, navy and air force tried to get a foothold in Norway at Narvik but were forced to withdraw. This failure was a real shock to the nation, but worse was to come.

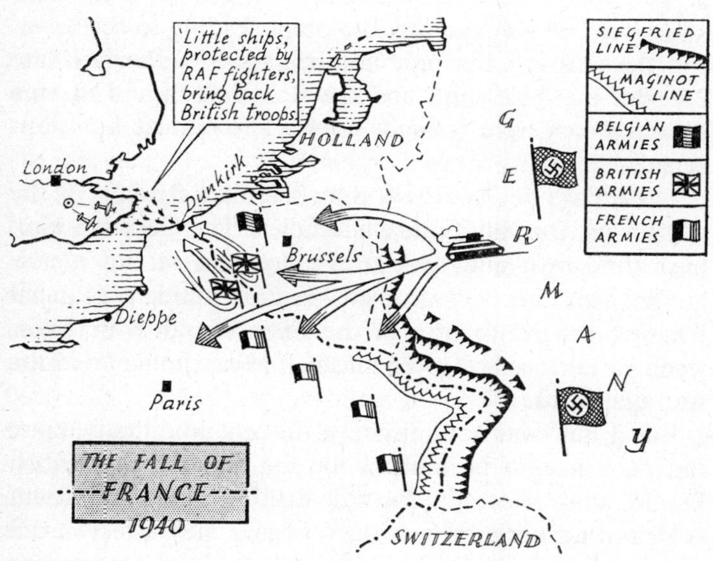

In May 1940 Hitler's forces attacked Holland and Belgium, moving round the north of the Maginot Line. The right part of the Allied armies stayed behind the Maginot Line. The left part, which included the British Expeditionary Force, the 'B.E.F.', marched north to meet the German troops. But the Germans pushed on, splitting the opposing armies in two, and the German tanks rumbled on into France. The B.E.F. and their French allies had only one way of escape, to the north, but this meant that all the troops, nearly 350,000 of them, would have to be taken off by sea. It seemed that only a miracle could save them, but a huge fleet of little ships and boats was hastily gathered together in English ports and sailed for the port of Dunkirk. There the beaches were packed with men, more were crowding along the roads leading to the town, and the German air force bombed them endlessly (Plate 23). But the little ships and the R.A.F. won and in nine days the men were brought home. The miracle had happened.

These days of June 1940 were the blackest days of the war for us. Our ally France had fallen. The Germans took over the north and west of France and set up a new government in 'Unoccupied France' under Marshal Pétain, an aged veteran of the First World War. Now, when Britain seemed to be finished, Mussolini entered the war against us.

But Britain was not finished, although, admittedly, there did not seem to be much hope for her. All the British Dominions—Australia, New Zealand, Canada and South Africa—had declared war on Germany just after we did and now the Commonwealth stood alone against the strength of Germany and Italy. The disasters of 1940 brought the end of Neville Chamberlain's government, and a new National Government was formed from men of all parties under Winston Churchill. Churchill proved to be the strong leader needed in time of danger. He did not promise that things would be easy: he promised only 'blood, tears, toil and sweat' before victory was won.

Britain became the headquarters of governments whose countries had been overrun: Holland, Norway, Poland, Czechoslovakia. Many Frenchmen disagreed with Marshal Pétain's government at Vichy and wanted to carry on the fight against Hitler. The leader of these 'Free French' or 'Fighting French' was General de Gaulle, who had his headquarters in Britain too.

AIR-RAID WARNING!

At this time Hitler offered to make peace if we would let him keep all his conquests, but Britain and the Commonwealth countries refused. So Hitler now had to try to conquer Britain, and in August 1940 the 'Battle of Britain' began. This was not a battle between armies but the desperate struggle of a few R.A.F. fighter pilots against the bombers and fighters of Hitler's *Luftwaffe*. London was the main target for German bombs, but many other places were attacked and horribly damaged: Portsmouth, Plymouth, Coventry, Liverpool and Clydebank. It seemed impossible that Britain could survive such attacks, but the fighter pilots went up day after day and many of them gave their lives. As Churchill said, 'Never in the field of human conflict was so much owed by so many to so few.'

We held out in the air—and we held out at sea too. The U-boats attacked our merchant ships more heavily than in the 1914–1918 war: and this danger to our food supplies was fought by crews of R.A.F. Coastal Command and the Royal Navy, using new weapons developed by scientists. All this time President Roosevelt urged his country to help Britain as far as possible. The slogan of the main political parties of the U.S.A. was 'all aid for Britain short of war'. The U.S.A. gave Britain fifty old destroyers in June 1940; and soon a flood of American arms began to pour across the Atlantic under the 'Lend-Lease' arrangement, which enabled us to have the arms although we could not pay for them.

Meanwhile the Battle of Britain went on from the summer of 1940 to the summer of 1941. To make matters worse, the armies in North Africa were pushed back by General Rommel almost to the River Nile. Then the strain on British civilians was made a little easier because Hitler now felt strong enough to make war on Russia. His armies swept on until they reached the great cities of Leningrad, Stalingrad and Moscow. Towards the end of 1941 it looked as if Hitler was just about to deal the death blows to Britain and her new ally, Russia. Now, just as Italy had joined Hitler in our darkest days of 1940, so

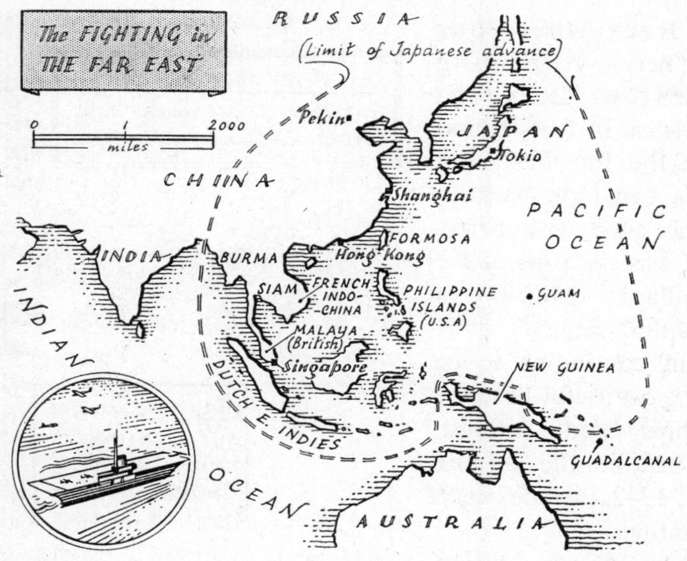

Japan joined Germany and Italy in time (so she thought) for the 'kill'.

Japan thought that Italy and Germany would conquer Britain and Russia, and she tried to deal a knock-out blow to the U.S. Navy. This, she believed, would enable her to build a new Japanese empire in the Far East. So, without even declaring war, on December 7th, 1941, her bombers attacked the biggest base of the American Pacific Fleet at Pearl Harbour. This was perhaps the real turning-point of the war, for it brought America in on the Allied side. Japan did enormous damage at Pearl Harbour and her troops swept on through the Philippines, the East Indies, Malaya, Singapore and Burma until they were at the doorstep of Australia.

Everywhere our armies were being beaten: in North Africa, in Russia, and in the Far East. But we can look back to this time with pride. It was the time of the gallant defence of Malta, bombed daily but continuing to be a most useful base for ships and aircraft. Then, in the autumn of 1942, the tide began to turn.

In North Africa, Field-Marshal Alexander and Field-Marshal Montgomery struck at General Rommel's troops at El Alamein. The Eighth Army, including the armoured division called the 'Desert Rats,' chased Rommel's army across the Western Desert, across Libya and Tunisia through the ports of Tobruk and Benghazi. All the way the German and Italian forces were attacked by the bombers and fighters of the Desert Air Force. Meanwhile, a large British and American army under General Eisenhower had landed in Algeria and Morocco and the retreating Germans

Nov. 8th–12th 1942. British and American forces under Gen. Eisenhower land in N. Africa.
Gibraltar
Casablanca
Oran
Algiers
MOROCCO
ALGERIA
May 1943. German & Italian troops, driven back to Tunisia, surrender there.
NORTH AFRICA 1942–3
0
500 mls.

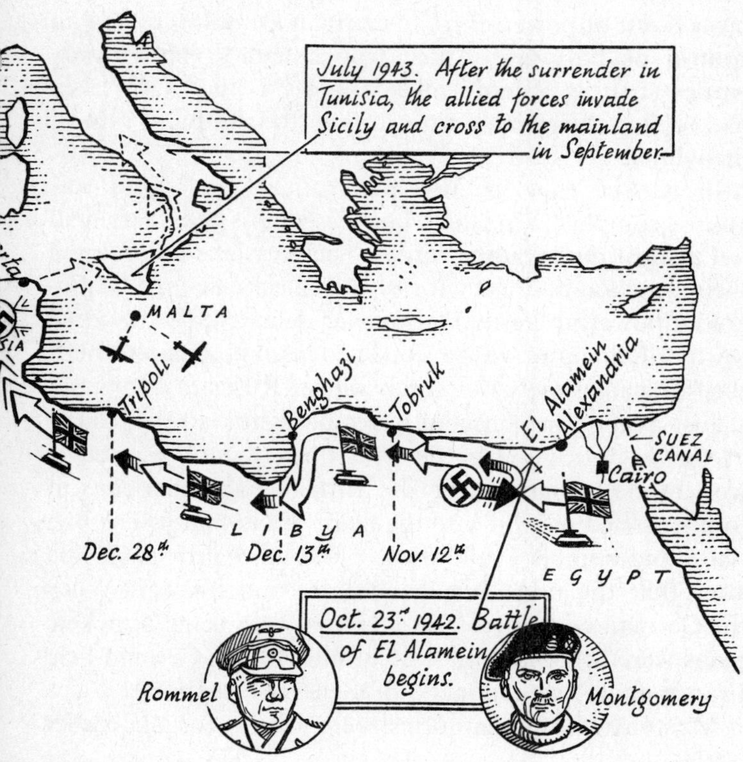

found themselves between this First Army and the Eighth Army. They were trapped: they could not escape by sea because of the might of the Allied navy and air force. In May 1943 three hundred thousand Germans and Italians surrendered to our forces.

In the following months the Allies conquered Sicily and prepared to invade the Italian mainland. By now the Italians had tired of Mussolini: he was disgraced and pushed out of power. But the German armies were now in control of Italy and Allied troops had to fight costly battles such as Salerno and Monte Cassino. Then they had to slog their way northwards in the mud and rain of the winter.

In Russia, too, the tide had turned. Stalingrad was almost completely in ruins, but the gallant defenders held out against the invading forces. The Russians reorganised their armies and arms factories and struck back. At Stalingrad a powerful German army was defeated; the besieged town of Leningrad was saved. The Russians began to push the Germans slowly but surely out of Russia.

Just as the wars on land were successful, so the 'Battle of the Atlantic', the battle with the U-boats, was being won too. And in the air the British and American air forces carried the war into the heart of Germany. The first 'thousand-bomber' raid took place in April 1942 and after that the raids became heavier and heavier. While the German coal mines and factories were being attacked, plans were being laid for a great invasion of German-held France under the command of General Eisenhower.

Most careful preparations were made, for an earlier

Canadian raid on Dieppe had shown how strong the coastal defences were. On 'D-Day', June 6th, 1944, the British and American forces landed on the Normandy beaches under an 'umbrella' of fighter aircraft and fire from naval vessels (see Plate 27). Two great artificial 'Mulberry' harbours were towed across, and later an underwater pipeline (with the code-name of 'Pluto'!) carried fuel oil from England to France.

There was heavy fighting for several weeks. Then, while the British and Canadians held most of the enemy tanks at bay, the Americans on the right broke through and began to encircle thousands of German troops. The Germans tried to retreat across the River Seine and the Allies swept on, freed north and west France and moved fast into Belgium and Holland. By September 1944 the Allies had reached the Rhine. Paratroopers were sent over the river to land at Arnhem in Holland, but the attempt failed in very bad weather. On the eastern front, the Russians were pushing on. They had cleared the Germans out of Finland, Bulgaria and Rumania

D-DAY, 1944

and were moving into Czechoslovakia, Hungary and Yugoslavia.

It seemed that the days of Hitler were almost ended. But he still hoped to break Britain. His 'V' or 'Victory' weapons were flying-bombs, sent towards London from firing-places in the Low Countries. The first type was the 'V1', but even more dangerous was the 'V2', a rocket-weapon which was faster than sound. London and Londoners suffered new wounds from these weapons, but they did not take Hitler any nearer to victory.

The spring of 1945 saw the end of the war in Europe. In the west the British and American forces were ready for the last battles over the Rhine. In the east the Russians were ready to take Berlin. Germany was in a scissors-hold. In May the two armies met at Leipzig; Hitler (as far as we know) killed himself in an air-raid shelter, and Germany surrendered. May 8th was VE-Day—the day of Victory in Europe.

Germany and Italy were both out of the war, Hitler and Mussolini were both dead, but Japan held out. British troops, the Fourteenth Army under General Slim, pushed the Japanese eastwards out of Burma in most difficult jungle fighting. American and Australian troops pushed the Japanese northwards away from Australia. Just before VE-Day American troops made a costly landing at Okinawa, about 300 miles from Japan. American 'Flying Fortresses' bombed Japanese cities, but the Emperor Hirohito's government held on. Obviously the fighting would have to be taken to Japan: but that might mean the sacrifice of thousands more lives.

President Truman was faced with an awful choice.

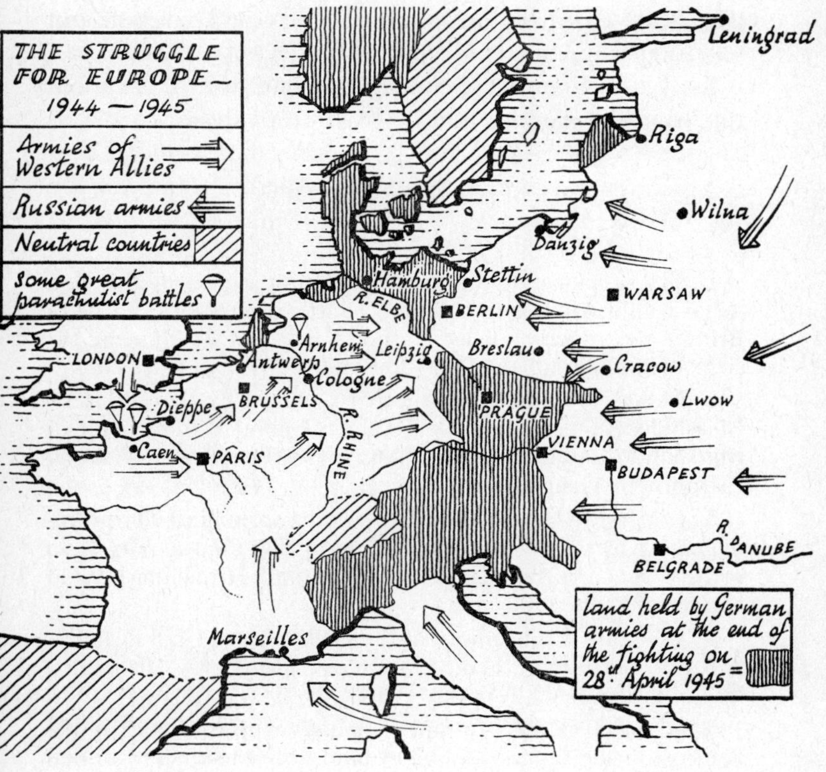

Should he send thousands more troops to their deaths? Or should he make use of a fearsome new weapon which would kill large numbers of civilians and injure many more? The decision was made: the first atom bomb was dropped on the city of Hiroshima, and three days later another was dropped on Nagasaki. This was on the 6th and 9th of August, and on 8th August the Russians declared war on Japan. Japan felt she could not hold out any longer and surrendered on 15th August, 'VJ-Day'.

Six years of war were ended. Men had now to set about repairing the damage and destruction of these years.

THINGS TO DO

Note: Plates 22–28 illustrate this chapter

1. Try to pick out the most important events of the war. What would you add to this list?—Battle of Dunkirk; Battle of Britain; the attack on Pearl Harbour; Battle of El Alamein; the siege of Stalingrad; the first thousand-bomber raid; D-Day.

2. Make sure you know the parts played by these leaders: Marshal Pétain, General de Gaulle, General Rommel, Field-Marshal Alexander and Field-Marshal Montgomery, General Eisenhower, General Slim.

3. Make a list of all the places we have mentioned and remember why they were so important during the war. To begin with, where are Arnhem, El Alamein and Hiroshima? What happened at these places?

4. What are the meanings of these: *Blitzkrieg*, Civil Defence, A.R.P., *Luftwaffe*, 'Lend-Lease' aid, 'Mulberry' harbours, 'Pluto', V1 and V2, VE-Day, VJ-Day?

5. It should be easy to find somebody who took part in the fighting during the war on sea or land or in the air. Try to find out part of the story of the war first-hand.

6.

'*We shall fight*'

On June 4th, 1940, the last day of the retreat from Dunkirk, Prime Minister Churchill made a famous speech. He wanted to explain to the world that Britain was not going to surrender. This is what he said:

> 'We shall go on to the end. We shall fight in France, we shall fight in the seas and oceans, we shall fight with growing

confidence and growing strength in the air; we shall defend our Island, whatever the cost may be. We shall fight on the beaches, we shall fight on the landing-grounds, we shall fight in the fields and in the streets, we shall fight in the hills; we shall never surrender; and even if, which I do not for a moment believe, this Island or a large part of it were subjugated and starving, then our Empire beyond the seas, armed and guarded by the British fleet, would carry on the struggle, until, in God's good time, the New World, with all its power and might, steps forth to the rescue and the liberation of the Old.'

Copy into your notebook the words that seem to you to be the most thrilling.

27

The World after 1945

JUST remember what had happened by the time of the end of the war in Europe. Mussolini's Roman Empire and Hitler's Greater Reich had both been overthrown by hard fighting. Mussolini had been shot by a Communist firing-squad and Hitler had killed himself in an air-raid shelter. The danger from these two dictators was ended, but they left Europe and the world with many problems.

What were these problems? First, the world was sick of war. People wanted to be sure that any quarrels between nations would be settled peacefully and not by force. The League of Nations, set up after the First World War, had failed and the world had lost faith in it. So a new 'League' was begun, the United Nations Organisation or UNO. It was born in 1945 and it has its headquarters at Lake Success near New York. There were fifty member-nations at first, and now there are over seventy. All these members have signed the Charter of the United Nations, in which they declare that they are 'determined to save succeeding generations from the scourge of war, which twice in our lifetime has brought untold sorrow to mankind'.

The United Nations Organisation has a kind of parliament which meets every year to discuss important matters affecting the peace and happiness of the world. Every member-nation sends five representatives to the Assembly, but the five have only one vote between them. This big Assembly cannot do all the day-to-day work and so there

THE UNITED NATIONS HEADQUARTERS

are many committees and organisations inside UNO. Perhaps the most important of these committees is the Security Council, which tries to settle any quarrel between nations that might lead to war. The Security Council has eleven members; one from each of the biggest countries—Britain, China, France, Russia and the U.S.A.—and six other members chosen by the Assembly. Any smaller quarrel which needs the decision of judges is settled by the International Court of Justice which sits at The Hague in Holland with fifteen judges from different countries. This was not a new Court, but was now made part of UNO.

REFUGEES

But it was not enough just to settle quarrels between nations. The war had left broken towns, broken trade and broken people. In many countries whole cities lay in ruins. Trade and industry were everywhere interrupted and in some places at a standstill. In Britain food was rationed, but there was enough to keep us in health. In other countries thousands of people were starving wanderers, without homes and without hope.

The United Nations came to the rescue. Medicines, doctors, nurses, food, tents, clothing, were sent to peoples who needed them. Once this sort of help was given, these countries had to start earning their living again. The factories had to be rebuilt, the mines put in order and struggling industries had to be encouraged. This time the richest Western nation came to the rescue. The U.S.A., through its Secretary of State, Mr. Marshall, promised money and raw materials and this 'Marshall Plan' helped many European countries to get back to normal life.

* * *

But already in 1947 it was clear that the dream of Robert Burns had not come true,

That man to man the world o'er,
Shall brithers be for a' that.

Russia was suspicious of Western nations and showed it in several ways. First, she would only join UNO if she, and the other Great Powers, were given the power of the 'veto' in the Security Council: that is, the power to stop some action they did not like. The other Powers were so anxious to have Russia in the United Nations that they agreed. Since then, Russia has used this power many times to stop the Western countries doing things they wanted to do. Second, Russia would not agree to Germany being united again. Today there is a Western Germany with its capital at Bonn, and an Eastern Germany which is Communist like Russia. Because of the constant danger from the huge Russian army, the countries of Western

Europe, Canada and the U.S.A. formed an alliance called the North Atlantic Treaty Organisation (NATO) to defend themselves in case of an attack by Russia.

So the war which overthrew Fascist and Nazi dictators left Communist dictators stronger than ever before. There are Communist governments in East Germany, Hungary,

THE HUNGARIAN RISING, 1956

Czechoslovakia, Bulgaria, Rumania, Yugoslavia, Poland, Estonia, Latvia, and Lithuania. Most of these are 'satellites': that is, they follow the policy laid down by Moscow. Some are more independent: President Tito of Yugoslavia often disagreed with the men of the Kremlin; and since 1956 Poland has been less under the control of Moscow. But Russia has shown that she is not prepared to let this independence go too far. In November 1956 there was a rebellion in Hungary against the pro-Russian government and officials. It was put down only when Russian tanks rumbled in from the east and brutally crushed the rebels. Unfortunately, Russia is still suspicious of the West, but we are always hoping that feelings will improve and that the 'Iron Curtain' will be lifted.

* * *

In other parts of the world there were great problems too. In Japan the Emperor Hirohito remained on his throne but his country was occupied by forces, mainly American, under General MacArthur. The Japanese people were taught not to look upon their Emperor as a kind of god, and a freer kind of government was set up. Japan's trade quickly improved, and she is prospering.

In China the Nationalist government of General Chiang Kai-shek was overthrown by Communist armies helped by Russia. China became a Communist country and the Nationalists were driven back to the island of Formosa, where they were helped and supplied by the U.S.A.

In 1950 alarming things happened in this part of the world. The Communists, who were strong in North Korea, marched south to force the South Koreans to turn Communist. The United Nations decided to stop this Communist attack, and an army made up of troops from many countries took part. Fighting went on for many months, but in the end the United Nations army kept South Korea free from Communism.

The U.N. had to interfere in another dispute in 1956.

A war broke out between Israel and Egypt, and Britain and France intervened to save the Suez Canal, fearing that the U.N. would not act quickly enough. Egyptian defences were bombed and allied paratroopers landed. Because of this the U.N. was stirred to act quickly and an international force was sent to keep the peace between Egypt and Israel.

* * *

Meanwhile, what was happening in the Commonwealth? Canada, Australia and New Zealand, while looking after their own affairs as self-governing Dominions, remained firm members of the family of nations. However, like Britain, they are finding that they must also work closely with the U.S.A. in matters of trade and defence.

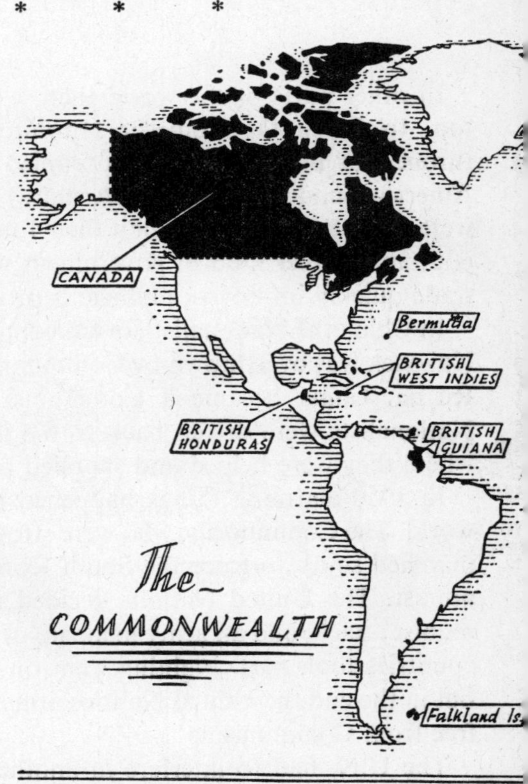

In other parts of the Commonwealth great changes have taken place. In the Union of South Africa, Field-Marshal Smuts, a Prime Minister who was an old and good friend of Britain, was defeated by the Nationalist party led by Dr. Malan in the election of 1949. Dr. Malan's government aims eventually to take South Africa out of the Commonwealth and set up a Republic. It also thinks the increasing coloured population is a danger to the 'white man', and is trying

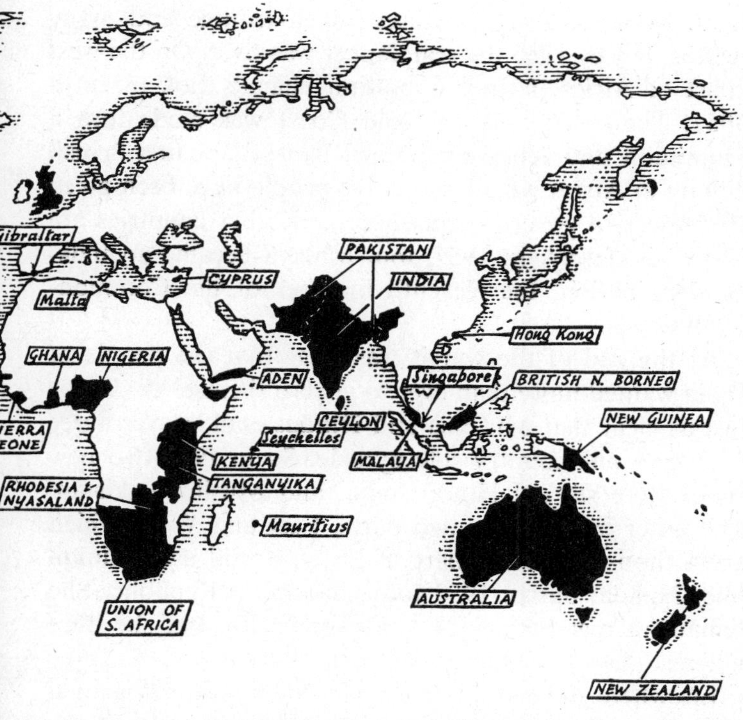

to separate white and coloured people in various ways. It calls this policy *apartheid*. It is taking away full voting rights from the coloured folk; it is making them live in separate districts, and it is preventing them from working in certain occupations.

In Kenya some members of the fine Kikuyu tribe were very jealous of the white settlers who, they said, had taken their land. So they formed a secret society called the Mau Mau to kill white people and force them to leave Kikuyu land. Mau Mau gangs caused much trouble and many deaths, but by 1956 the real danger was over. On the west coast of Africa, a very important change took place in 1957. The colony of the Gold Coast was made into a Dominion and renamed Ghana. This is the first British colony in Africa where the native people have been given the power to govern themselves, and other countries are watching closely. In 1957, too, Malaya became an independent nation, the eleventh member of the Commonwealth.

At the end of the war it was clear that the people of India wanted more than ever to govern themselves. It was just as clear that Muslims and Hindus could never agree to live in one country side by side. So in 1947 two new states were set up: Hindu India, and Muslim Pakistan. The latter is split into two parts, East and West, which are a thousand miles apart. Pakistan is still a Dominion like Canada, but in 1950 India became a Republic. She remains a member of the Commonwealth, but she does not recognise our Queen as Queen of India.

Elsewhere, former French and Dutch colonies gained full independence too. After some bitter fighting the Dutch

East Indies became the Republic of Indonesia. In French Indo-China the states of Tonkin and Amman became the Republic of Viet Nam.

* * *

So the world after 1945, although it was at peace, was full of problems. In Europe, there is the Iron Curtain which we hope will be raised when there is greater trust between East and West. In Asia, new nations have arisen which have their own lives to shape. In the Commonwealth, new ideas are at work. It is no longer an Empire ruled by Britain, but a family of nations. We hope that these Commonwealth countries and their friends will be able to work through UNO for a better world.

THINGS TO DO

1. Write a short paragraph on UNO, mentioning the Charter, the Security Council and the International Court of Justice. Find out more about the work of other parts of UNO, such as UNICEF (the United Nations International Children's Emergency Fund) and WHO (the World Health Organisation).
2. What do these mean: 'Marshall Plan', the 'veto', 'satellite' country, the 'Iron Curtain', *apartheid*?
3. Study a map of the world in 1939 and compare it with a map of the world today. What are the main differences?
4. Is this chapter out of date now? What important events have taken place in the world since it was written?
5. Who are the leading statesmen today in the countries we have read about? Make as complete a list as you can.

28

From the Stone Age to Our Own

Now we have followed the story of men from very earliest times to our own day. There has not been time to read about everything, of course, and there is a great deal more to know. In the next book we will learn about some of these things: about what is happening at home, in the Commonwealth of Nations, and in other lands. In other words, we will try to find out all we can about the world in which you will live and work when you leave school.

Just now, though, let us look back. Let us see how our world compares with the world our forefathers knew at different times.

One of the first things we spoke about was the struggle that early men had to find the things they needed most—food, clothing and shelter. Remember how slowly and

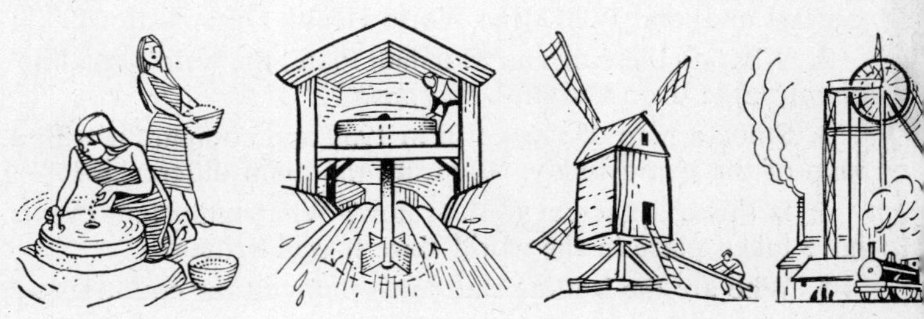

painfully men and women discovered better ways of doing things. Nowadays we do not all try to find or make everything we require: we specialise in doing one thing and are paid for it. With the money we earn we pay builders and tailors and farmers and others to provide the things we need.

Once men started to specialise on one job or trade progress was much quicker. Still better ways of producing things were found. Now we still wear woven clothes made of wool but the huge looms of our textile factories would scare the wits of Stone Age women who spun their wool by hand and wove it on their rough upright looms.

Men have learned about the wonders of this world we live in and have learned to harness the power that is in Nature. They discovered that there were better ways of spinning and of grinding corn than doing it by hand. They learned of the power that lies in wind and water and began to build windmills and water mills. Later they learned of the power that lies in a jet of steam. Later still they found out about the electricity in the atmosphere and we are still learning new ways of making it for ourselves. Nature has provided us with power and men have learned to use

POWER THROUGH THE AGES

the treasure locked up in the earth: copper and tin to make bronze, iron, coal, oil, and now uranium for atomic power.

Using the power of Nature and the minerals of the earth, then, men have made machines to do work and to make things for them. These power-driven machines, looked after by a few men, do the work of hundreds of men and make things much more cheaply and quickly than by the old methods. With these 'servants' working for us, we can afford to have in our homes things that our forefathers did not have. Many of these things were not even invented in your grandfather's young days.

So, thanks to scientists and engineers, we have countless machines working for us and we have comfortable homes. In a great many other ways our lives are much better than those of our forefathers. Parliament has been changed and now even the poorest men and women have the vote and can help to choose their government. In the last century Parliament has passed all kinds of Acts to help ordinary folk: Factory Acts, Acts to help Trade Unions, Health Acts, Education Acts and many others. Now your parents do not have to pay school fees and do not have to pay the doctor every time he visits you. If your father falls ill or is out of work, he receives health or unemployment 'benefit' until he works again.

Of course all these things have to be paid for. Your father helps to pay when insurance stamps are bought out of his wages every week. More money comes from taxes—income tax, purchase tax, entertainment tax, and so on. This means that everybody helps those who need help—whether they are sick or unemployed or old or widows or orphans. So nowadays there is not the poverty and starvation that there used to be. Nor, thanks to the work of doctors and chemists, is there the ill-health and disease that used to be so common.

* * *

All this peaceful progress should make us very thankful and very grateful to the men and women of many nation-

THEY NEED OUR HELP

alities and many centuries whose work has made it possible. But there are other sides to this happy picture.

Many countries are not as fortunate as we are in Britain. In Asia and Africa, particularly, millions of people need help. They need money, doctors and medicines, farm implements and seed, to make their own lands happier and healthier. You will have heard in your geography lessons about such countries and their struggles today.

It is not certain that we in Britain will be able to go on raising our comforts and standard of living or even keep up the comfortable standards that we have now. If we do not use fully the machines and the skill of our people, we will not earn the money that our country needs to buy food from abroad. We are many people in a small land and we have to work hard and work together to earn our living.

Some people do not realise how important it is for everybody to pull his weight—not only in his or her work, but in the government of the country too. Many people do not use their vote in elections and do not take an interest in how the country is governed. Where this happens it is possible for a few men to take control and do things that many of their people do not want. You have read about the dictators of recent times, between the Great Wars.

It is all the more tragic that many people do not take an interest in how the country is governed, because the work of governments is becoming more and more important. It is part of a government's work to keep friendly with other countries and not to do anything that might lead to war, for there has been 'progress' in making war too. From spears and bows and arrows men have learned more terrible ways of killing each other until now we are frightened by the latest inventions. Scientists have made it possible for us to reach New York in hours instead of days or even weeks. But they have also made it possible for atomic weapons to be fired from one country to another hundreds of miles away to kill thousands of people

SCIENCE IN WAR AND PEACE

there. The world seems a smaller, but more dangerous, place.

But we want to go on making progress, using scientific discoveries to help us and to help us to help others. We want to have a world where nations are friendly with each other and are not afraid for their lives; and where poorer nations are given help. This was the dream of the League of Nations and now of UNO.

Throughout history men have learned that progress is possible only if they work together in peace. Today we want to keep the peace and to protect what we value more than anything else—our freedom to live the life we choose for ourselves. Take an interest in history as it unfolds in the years ahead—and play your part.

BBC
DAILY · NEWS
PICTURE WEEKLY
SCRAP BOOK

Index